The

PRACTICAL
EXPRESSION

of the Church

Witness Lee

LIVING STREAM MINISTRY
Anaheim, California • www.lsm.org

© 1970 Living Stream Ministry

First Edition, 1970.

ISBN 978-0-87083-015-0

Published by

Living Stream Ministry
2431 W. La Palma Ave., Anaheim, CA 92801 U.S.A.
P. O. Box 2121, Anaheim, CA 92814 U.S.A.

Printed in the United States of America

11   12   13   14   15   16 / 13   12   11   10   9   8   7   6

CONTENTS

4   THE PRACTICAL EXPRESSION OF THE CHURCH

PREFACE

This book is composed of messages given by Brother Witness Lee during the 1968 summer conference and training meetings in Los Angeles, California.

CHAPTER ONE

THE ETERNAL PURPOSE OF GOD

My burden in these chapters is to share with you something regarding the practical expression of the church. Regarding Christ, we need living experience, and concerning the church, we must have a practical expression.

THE CHURCH
PURPOSED IN ETERNITY

Ephesians 3:10-11 unveils the fact that the existence of the church is according to the eternal purpose of God which He made in Christ. The church is something of God's eternal purpose. It did not come into existence by accident but was planned in eternity. Before time began, in eternity, God purposed to have the church.

The word *purpose* here in the Scriptures is equivalent to the word *plan*. God's eternal purpose is God's eternal plan. God has a plan which He planned in eternity—He is not purposeless; He is a God of purpose.

What did God plan? He planned to have a church composed of a group of human beings coordinated together as a corporate Body with which He may mingle Himself in His divine nature. In other words, this corporate Body would be a corporate vessel, into which He would put Himself. This is the very thing God planned, and this is the very center of His purpose. God planned to have a corporate Body, a corporate vessel, with which He could mingle Himself and all that He is. This vessel is called the church.

The church, therefore, is the center of God's eternal plan. Why is the church so dear, so lovable, and so precious to God? It is because the church is the desire of God's heart, which He purposed before time began. God in eternity planned to have the church.

ALL THINGS ARE FOR THE CHURCH

The full revelation of the Scripture reveals to us that all things in the universe are for the church. Even the three persons of the Godhead are for the divine purpose of having a church to fulfill God's eternal plan.

We are all familiar with the three persons of the Godhead: God the Father, God the Son, and God the Spirit. These three persons of the Godhead do not exist so that we may have a doctrine of the Trinity but are for the accomplishment of God's plan to produce the church. They are for the dispensing of God Himself into humanity in order that the church may come into existence.

Some men have little purpose; therefore, their appearance is continually the same. But a man full of purpose may have several appearances. If you could visit him at his home in the early hours of the day, you would see that he is a father or a husband. After breakfast, he may go to a university to be a professor. Then at the hospital in the afternoon, you may see him in a white uniform as a doctor. At home he is a father, in the university he is a professor, and in the hospital he is a doctor. Why is he these three kinds of persons? Because he is a man of great purpose.

Do not think that because there are three persons in the Godhead, there are three separate Gods. No, They are absolutely one. Matthew 28:19 says that we are to baptize people into *the name* of the Father and of the Son and of the Spirit. There are three persons but only *one name*. It is not into the *names* of the Father, the Son, and the Spirit, but into the *name*. The father in the home, the professor in the university, and the doctor in the hospital are also three persons with one name.

Consider electricity. The same electricity stored in the generator is also installed in many buildings. How can the electricity in the generator be installed in buildings miles away? It is by the current of electricity. But is the current of electricity something other than electricity itself? No, the current of electricity is simply electricity in motion. When we apply electricity to the lights, the heater, the air conditioner, or many other appliances, it is still electricity, but it has come in three stages—the electricity stored in the generator, the electricity transmitted into the building by its current, and the electricity applied to various appliances. Are these three kinds of electricity? No, they are simply one electricity in three stages, and the purpose of these stages is that the electricity might be dispensed and applied.

There is one God in three persons for the purpose of dispensing and applying God to us. God the Father is the source of the heavenly electricity; God the Son is the current of the heavenly electricity; and God the Spirit is the application, the function, of the heavenly electricity. Thus, God Himself can be dispensed into us and applied so that the church may be produced and exist. For the producing and existence of the church, God must be in three persons. The dispensing of the Godhead is much more important than the teaching of the Trinity.

In order that the church may exist in this universe to express God, the heavens, the earth, space, and a multitude of other items are required. Without these things God could never have a church in the universe to express Himself. God is in three persons for the church. God created billions of creatures for the church. Everything is for the church, and everything is because of the church.

For the producing of the church, there is also the need of a tripartite man, a man with three parts—spirit, soul, and body. This is indeed interesting. Not only is there the need of man, but of man in three parts, with a body, a soul, and a spirit. Why must man be in three parts? The body of man is related to the creation. The soul of man is related to man himself, and the spirit of man is related to God. Thus, there could be a church composed of man in the universe.

Without God in three persons, without the creation of so many things, and without man in three parts, it is impossible for the church to come into existence. For the purpose of having the church, all these are necessary. God, creation, and man are all for the church; so eventually we see that the church is the center, the kernel, of God's eternal plan.

THE ECONOMY OF THE MYSTERY

In Ephesians 3:9-11 many great and significant terms are used because they are related to God's eternal plan. We must all know the economy of God's mystery. This mystery has been hidden in God for generations from the beginning of creation. Even before the foundation of the world, God was exceedingly clear regarding this mystery.

All the creatures do not know this mystery. It has been hidden in God. If you could ask a tiger or a lion why they are here, they would tell you that they do not know. If you were to ask university professors the meaning of life, I believe they all would answer that they simply do not know.

But praise the Lord! This mystery has been made known. We know why God is in three persons. We know why the creation of the heavens and the earth and so many billions of items is necessary and why mankind was brought into existence. We know because God has made known to us this mystery. We know what the economy of the mystery is, which has been hidden in God from the beginning of the creation. *It is all for the church.*

THE DISPLAY OF GOD'S MULTIFARIOUS WISDOM

With this eternal purpose of God, God's multifarious wisdom is shown; and it is made known not only to man but to the rulers and the authorities in the heavenlies. God makes a display of His wisdom to all these angelic powers through the church. Hallelujah, this is real wisdom! It is made known through the church, not through individuals. This is why we all must respect the church and realize how much we need the church. As long as we are in the church, it is a glory to God and a shame to the enemy. But as long as we are out of the church, it is a shame to God and a kind of boast to the enemy. We must have the church.

We are chosen, redeemed, saved, and regenerated not for heaven but *for the church.* The church is God's goal. The church is God's aim. The church is the center of God's plan.

GIFTED PERSONS AND THE CHURCH

Ephesians 4:11-12 tells us that all the gifted persons—the apostles, prophets, evangelists, and shepherds and teachers—are for the church. They are for the perfecting of the saints, that the building up of the church may be realized.

It is indeed regrettable that today so many so-called Christian workers, ministers, and teachers are doing a work without much regard for the church. They only care for their work; they care little for the church. The work they are doing, in a sense, is frustrating, destroying, and damaging the church. All the gifted persons must be for the church. To be an apostle must be for the church. To be a prophet must be for the church. To be an evangelist must be for the church. To be a shepherd and teacher must be for the church. Whatever the Lord commits to us or burdens us to do must be for the church. The church is what God is after. The church is what God planned and desires to have.

THE BEGINNING AND THE END

There are two important verses spoken by the Lord in the New Testament regarding the church. One is at the beginning of the New Testament in the book of Matthew, and the other is at the end in the book of Revelation. The first time the word *church* is used is by the Lord in Matthew 16:18. In this verse and its context (vv. 16-17, 19) we see three things which are related to one another: Christ, the church, and the kingdom. Whenever Christ is revealed to man, immediately the church must come into view. The church can only be produced by knowing Christ, and the church must be produced by the realization of Christ. After Peter came to know Christ, immediately the Lord Jesus said that He would build His church, against which the gates of Hades would not prevail.

Then following the church, the kingdom is mentioned. Christ produces the church, and the church brings in the kingdom. Where Christ is realized, the church is produced. Then the church will bring in the kingdom, the reign, and the authority of God on the earth. Therefore, the church is the key.

The Lord is the Alpha, and He is also the Omega. He speaks something about the church in the *first* book of the New Testament, and then in the *last* book, as a consummation of the whole Bible, He speaks to the churches about the church. The book of Revelation is not written to individuals but to the local churches. "I am the Alpha and the Omega" (1:8) and "What you see write in a scroll and send it to the seven churches" (v. 11).

If we are outside the local churches, we have no position or standing to take the book of Revelation, for it was not written to individual believers. It was written to the local churches, though the Lord called individual believers to listen to it. We must be in the local church; then we are qualified with the position and standing to accept this book and listen to what the Lord Spirit speaks to His churches.

The Lord Jesus never forgets what He begins. We may forget, but He never forgets. In the first book of the New Testament, He spoke about the building of the church, and what He began He will accomplish. He is the Alpha and the Omega, the beginning and the end, to accomplish the building up of the church.

In the beginning He spoke about the universal church, but practically speaking, when He comes to the end, it is the local churches. The Lord begins with the church, and He ends with the churches. The church is universal, and the churches are local. The local churches are more practical to us than the universal church. The local churches are the accomplishment of the universal church. God needs the local churches to fulfill His eternal purpose of the universal church.

May our eyes be opened to see the economy of the mystery according to God's eternal purpose which He purposed before the beginning of creation. We must see the church according to the eternal plan which God planned in Christ in eternity.

CHAPTER TWO

THE EXPRESSION OF CHRIST

We have seen the purpose of God in chapter 1, and we must now see the expression of Christ. God planned the church for the purpose of expressing Christ; thus, the church is the expression of Christ. But how can the church be the expression of Christ? In what way can the church express Christ? The only way is by the church being the Body of Christ.

THE CHURCH—THE BODY OF CHRIST

If you consider yourself, you will realize that your body is your expression. Without a body we cannot express ourselves. In like manner, there is no way for Christ to be expressed by the church except by it being His Body. In saying that the body is the expression, we must realize that the body is always one with the head in life and in nature. Our body is one life and one nature with our head. This tells us that the church is one with Christ in life and nature. In other words, according to life and nature, Christ is the church. Christ is not only the Head, but He is also the Body, because the Body's life is Christ, and the Body's nature is Christ. The Body is Christ, and Christ is the Body.

In the Bible there is an excellent type regarding Christ and the church. It is the type of Adam and Eve. Strictly speaking, God did not create a man and a woman; He only created one man. Then how did the woman come into being? The wife was just a part of the husband. God put Adam to sleep, broke his side, and took out a rib. This was a part of Adam, and this part became his wife.

What, then, was Eve? Eve was only a part of Adam. Therefore, it is absolutely right to say that Adam was Eve, because

Eve was a part of Adam. We all know, according to Ephesians 5, that this is a type. Christ was the last Adam, and God put Him to sleep on the cross. His side was broken, and out of His side came blood and water (John 19:34). Blood signifies redemption, and water signifies life. Both are needed to produce the spiritual Eve, the spiritual bride, which is the church.

We need this vision and revelation to see what the church is. The church is simply the counterpart of Christ. The church is a part of Christ, a product of Christ. She is something that came out of Christ, something produced of Christ, and something which is a part of Christ. The Body can never be separated from the Head. A complete person has both a head and a body.

Today the church is simply the Body to Christ, a Body that is produced out of Christ and a Body that is part of Christ. This is why Ephesians 1:22-23 tells us that the church is the Body, and the Body is the fullness of Christ. Christ is the One who fills all in all. He is universally great, and this universally great Christ needs a Body to be His fullness, His expression.

THE RICHES OF CHRIST
AND THE FULLNESS OF CHRIST

In Ephesians 1:23, we have "the fullness of the One who fills all in all." This means the fullness of Christ. Then in Ephesians 3:8 we see "the unsearchable riches of Christ." What is the difference between the fullness of Christ and the riches of Christ? It is not difficult for us to realize the meaning of the riches of Christ. This must be all the items of what Christ is. As God He is the Father, the Son, the Spirit, the Lord, the Christ, and other items. As man Christ is the Apostle, the Teacher, and the Leader. He is really much more than this. He is our light, our life, our air, our water, our food, our clothing, and our lodging. He is all of this and more to us. There are countless items of the riches of Christ.

What then is the fullness? The fullness is the issue of the enjoyment of all the riches of Christ. When all the riches of Christ have been enjoyed and assimilated by us, then we will have the issue of the enjoyment of Christ's riches. The issue is the fullness of Christ.

I have used the riches of America to illustrate this many times: the milk, the cows, the eggs, the chickens, the peaches, the plums, and many other things are the riches of America, but the fullness of America is the issue of enjoying these riches.

For example, consider some men who are physically very large. In a sense they are not the riches of America but the fullness of the riches of America. How could they be so large? It is because they are composed of so many American chickens, cows, eggs, milk, and so forth.

All of you are the fullness of the riches of America. If you did not feed upon the riches of American food, you would all be greatly reduced. But since you are full of the riches of America, you all become the fullness of America. The fullness is the product of enjoying the riches. The more we enjoy the riches of this country, the more we become the fullness of this country.

What then is the church? The church is the fullness of Christ. This means that the church is the result of the enjoyment of the riches of Christ. We all must enjoy Christ. This is why we hate dead teachings and doctrines and prefer the enjoyment of Christ through pray-reading the Word. If we only learn the teachings and doctrines, it is just like learning the recipe and the menu without enjoying the food. It is better to forget the recipe and the menu and enjoy the riches of Christ. How rich He is, and how richly we can enjoy Him day by day! The more we enjoy Him, the more we will grow and become His fullness.

This is the expression. The fullness is the expression of Christ. We can never express Christ just by learning doctrines. We can never express Christ only by knowing the Bible. The adequate way for us to express Christ is to feed upon Him, eat of Him, drink of Him, and be filled with Him as our nourishment. We must take Him in and assimilate all that He is into our being. Then spontaneously, we will be His fullness, and this fullness is simply the expression of Christ.

This is the way for us to have a living expression of Christ. If the brothers and sisters in any church do not know how to feed upon Christ, how to enjoy Christ, and how to assimilate all that Christ is into their being, it is impossible to have a proper expression of the church in that locality. Teachings alone can never bring forth a proper expression of the church in any place. We must realize how much we need to feed on Christ, to enjoy Christ, to eat of Christ, and to drink of Christ. Then spontaneously, a proper expression of Christ will come into existence in our locality.

A local church is an expression of Christ, and this expression can only exist by taking Christ as our enjoyment. This is why I say again and again that we must enjoy Christ in such a practical and living way for ourselves. Then we can help others to enjoy Christ in the same way. Only in this way will we become the fullness, the expression, of Christ.

The essence, or substance, of the church must be Christ Himself assimilated into our being. This is very basic. If you do not know how to enjoy Christ, how to drink of Him, how to feed on Him, and how to take Him into your spirit and assimilate Him into your being, it is not possible for a proper local church to be produced in your locality.

Oneness is the first essential factor of a local church. If there is no oneness, there is no possibility of having a local expression of the church. Can we have oneness only by teachings? It is not possible to have oneness through teachings alone because throughout the centuries the more people learned just teachings, the more they were divided. We must pay more attention to the enjoyment of Christ than to the teachings. The more we enjoy Christ, the more we will be one. The more we feed upon Him, the more we are united.

I like what the apostle Paul says in Ephesians 3:8: "To me, less than the least of all saints, was this grace given to announce to the Gentiles the unsearchable riches of Christ." The apostle Paul did not preach the teachings or the doctrines, but the unsearchable riches of Christ. What is the purpose of the unsearchable riches of Christ? If we read verses 8 through 11, we will see that they are for the producing of the church. All the riches of Christ are simply for this one thing: to produce the church.

The more we partake of the riches of Christ, the more we realize that they are exceptionally rich. We all must learn day by day to enjoy these unsearchable riches; then we will know what we must minister to others. It should not be our intention to pass on teachings; we must be burdened simply to minister something of the riches of Christ to others.

I can never forget the lesson I learned in 1933 with Brother Watchman Nee. He did not talk with me about teachings and doctrines, but he helped me to enjoy Christ. He did not even use the word *enjoy,* but he helped me to enjoy Him. One day he asked me, "What is patience?" His question was so practical. I did not dare answer, for such a common question out of his mouth must be quite meaningful. But he forced me to tell him what I thought patience was. I then said that patience is the enduring of suffering or ill-treatment. When he told me that this is not patience, I was much bothered. If this is not patience, I thought, then what is patience? I asked him to tell me, but he would not, and we were together for a considerable length of time. When I asked him what patience was, he said, "Yes, what is patience?" This really disappointed me. I returned to the place where I stayed, and with tears I knelt down to ask the Lord to show me what patience is.

Within those days my eyes were opened. I saw that patience is Christ. Christ must be my patience. That was the key. Not only must my patience be Christ, but everything for me and to me must be Christ. It was through this one lesson that I learned how to take Christ as my patience, my humility, my love to others, and my everything. It was a real help to me.

Brother Nee did not give me any teaching. He ministered Christ to me as patience in a practical way, and it was not just one item, but one lesson which was the key to open the whole realm to me. By such a short, common sentence, he helped me eternally.

This is all we need. We do not need the mere teachings. Before I met Brother Nee, I received many teachings and doctrines from others. Though I sat at their feet for several years, it was not till that day when Brother Nee spoke with me that my eyes were opened. I saw that what I needed was not the teachings but the riches and the enjoyment of Christ.

Only the enjoyment of the riches of Christ can produce the

church. The church is not the product of teachings but something born of Christ. The church comes out of the enjoyment of the riches of Christ. It is part of Christ.

I have told people in many places that mere doctrines mean nothing as far as the church life is concerned, and in so doing, I have offended some. But I must say it. We must all be turned from doctrines to the riches of Christ in the Spirit, and we must be willing to be turned. If we are going to have a proper expression of the church in any locality, we need the real enjoyment of the riches of Christ.

THE BODY BEING CHRIST

We are told in 1 Corinthians 12:12 that the Body is Christ. Christ is the Body. The church is not composed of Americans, Japanese, Chinese, French, Germans, or British. The Body, which is the new man, has no Greek, no Jew, no circumcision, no uncircumcision, no barbarian, no Scythian, no civilized people, and no uncivilized people, but Christ is all and in all (Col. 3:11).

In the church there is only Christ. Christ is all in all. We all must be swallowed up by Christ. If there is only Christ, how can we have any opinions? If there is only Christ, how can we have any self-exalting factors? The divisions come from the different peoples, not from Christ.

In the Body, the expression of the church, there is only one person—Christ. We must enjoy Him and let Him swallow up all the different peoples. This is why in the church there is no Greek and no Jew, no cultured, and no barbarians. All are swallowed up by Christ, not by being taught but by being nourished with the riches of Christ.

We all need to see this clearly. When we go to any place, we must never try to correct or adjust others but only feed them with Christ. It is so easy to correct others, because we are so religious and trust so much in the teachings. But this will never work. We must guard ourselves from any temptation to correct others and simply show them how to enjoy Christ.

Suppose I am a person who is naturally very swift in all my actions, and I go to a certain place where all the people in the church are slow. I will immediately be tempted to correct them. Perhaps in the first two or three days I will exercise some patience, but it is only natural, human patience. After three days my patience will be exhausted, and I will utter something about their being so slow. *This is not the way.* We must only minister Christ to feed them. If Christ is the quicker One, Christ will do a quick job. If Christ is not so quick, then we must leave the matter to Christ. We should not adjust or correct but feed and nourish them with Christ. People do not need correction but the nourishment and the enjoyment of Christ.

THE CHURCH—THE HOUSE OF GOD
AND PILLAR OF THE REALITY

First Timothy 3:15-16 tells us that the church is the house of the living God. Only Christ Himself could be this house. Therefore, the church must be Christ. When we say that the local church is the house of God, we must realize that this house must be Christ. This house must not be a group of people but Christ alone. Only Christ can be the house of the living God.

In Ephesians 1:17-18 Paul says that our eyes must be opened so that we may see the hope of God's calling. This hope is Christ, and the riches of the glory of God's inheritance are simply the riches of Christ. The more we enjoy Christ and partake of Him, the more we will have the riches of the glory of Christ among us. This is the inheritance. God is going to inherit the Christ that is assimilated by the saints. The riches of Christ assimilated by the saints are God's inheritance, and this is the church. The church must be filled with the enjoyment of the riches of Christ; then we will have the riches of glory for God to inherit.

When Christ Himself is enjoyed by us, we will have the church as the real house of God and the pillar and base of the truth, the reality. Reality is Christ. Nothing on this earth or in this universe is real. Only Christ is the real One, the reality. So the church bears Christ as the reality. The church is the pillar and base to bear Christ and to show to the whole universe that everything is false but Christ. Everything is empty, but the reality is in the church. If you would know real love, come to the church. Christ is here as real love. If you would know real life, come to the church. Christ is here as real life. Christ is the reality. If you would see what faithfulness is, come to the church. The church has Christ as the real faithfulness, because the church bears Christ as the reality. If the church is not filled with Christ, how can the church bear Christ as the reality?

The church is also the manifestation of God in Christ. Here God is manifested, and this is the mystery of godliness. The church is a real mystery of godliness. Outwardly, the people may be of several races and nationalities, but inwardly, the church is Christ. Christ is in the church as the manifestation of God, and this is the mystery of godliness. This is the church.

The key point is that we all must enjoy Christ so that Christ can swallow us up. Then all that we are and have will simply be Christ. This is the essence and the substance of the church life. In the church we are the members of the Body (Rom. 12:4-5). We can never be independent or separated from the church. We must realize that we are a member of the Body wherever we go. How could we be a Christian without the Body, the church? As members of the Body, we do need the church life, and the church life is nothing but Christ Himself enjoyed by us and expressed in a corporate way.

CHAPTER THREE

THE EXPRESSION OF THE CHURCH

We have seen that the expression of Christ is the church. But how can the church be expressed? Christ is expressed through the church, but how is the church expressed? We must see the expression of the church which is the expression of Christ.

WHERE IS THE CHURCH?

Many people talk about the church as the expression of Christ, but after a little consideration we will ask, "Where is the church?" If we say that the church is the expression of Christ, then where is it? When people speak about the church as the expression of Christ, it sounds nice, but we must put nice things into practice. If you were to talk with me, I would reply, "Brother, it sounds good, but how can I get into it? It is marvelous that the church is the expression of Christ, but I would like to be in it. Tell me where it is."

If we were to ask this practical question to so many teachers who teach concerning the church as the expression of Christ, we would put them into the corner. Immediately, they would become embarrassed and entangled. They would be confused and find it difficult to answer.

The church as the expression of Christ is so heavenly, so spiritual, and so wonderful. But we want to get into it; we want to have it! Since it is so heavenly and so wonderful, where is it? Where can we find such a wonderful thing?

The teachers may tell us that it is too spiritual and that it is not something of this earth but in the heavens. If this is the case, it is impossible for the church to be in any locality on this earth, and we must conclude that we will have to wait for eternity. Thus, there is no reason for us to have the church today, and it is needless to talk about the things of the church today. If we must wait for eternity, it is unnecessary to care for the church now.

LOCAL CHURCHES

You see, this is the problem. People have seen just one aspect but not the other. Regarding the church, there are two terms in the Bible: "the church of God" (1 Cor. 10:32) and "the churches of God" (11:16). Is the church one or many? The church of God is universal, but the churches of God are expressed in so many localities.

The church is the expression of Christ, but how can the church be practically expressed? Only by the local churches, by one church in each locality. As the expression of Christ, the church is universally one, but it is expressed in many, many local churches.

The church could never be expressed without the local churches. Every local church is the practical expression of the church. This is why in Matthew 16:18 the Lord Jesus mentioned the building of the church upon the rock. But in Matthew 18:15-20 the Lord said something about the local church. The church mentioned in Matthew 18 must be a local church, because it is a place where we can go. The Lord said that if you have some problem with a brother, go to him first. If he listens to you, the problem is solved. But if he does not, you must bring one or two with you to witness to him, expecting him to listen to them. If he still does not listen, then you are to bring the problem to the church. Of course, this must be the local church. It could not be the universal church. We could never bring a problem to the universal church.

Suppose *you* have a problem with a brother. Do you have a church to go to? Is there a place in your locality where you can go? If not, there is no practical expression of the church in your city.

What is the practical expression of the church which is the expression of Christ? It is the local churches. Without local churches there is no possibility for the church to be expressed. Without local churches the church only becomes a kind of term; it becomes something in the heavens, something in the future, something for us to look forward to but not so real and practical today on this earth.

According to the Bible, however, the church is exceedingly practical. In Matthew 18 the Lord Jesus tells us that if we have a problem with a brother and it cannot be solved with two or three brothers, we must bring it to the church. There is no doubt that this is the local church in practicality.

Then in the book of Acts we immediately see the first expression of the church on the earth: "The church which was in Jerusalem" (8:1). It does not speak of the church in the heavens, but the church in Jerusalem. It is a local church, and this local church is the expression of the universal church. In Acts 13:1 there is the local church in Antioch. This is another expression of the church, another local church. Now we can see one church with at least two expressions: one is in Jerusalem; the other in Antioch. All local churches are the expressions of the one (universal) church.

As we continue through the New Testament, we see "the church which is in Cenchrea" (Rom. 16:1) and "the church of God which is in Corinth" (1 Cor. 1:2; 2 Cor. 1:1). The Bible never speaks of churches in one place but always of the church in a certain place—in other words, the church in Jerusalem, the church in Antioch, the church in Cenchrea, and the church in Corinth. Every local church is an expression of the one church. The church is one, but the expressions of the church are many, and these many expressions of the church are the local churches. "The churches of Judea" (Gal. 1:22; 1 Thes. 2:14), "the churches of the Gentiles" (Rom. 16:4), the churches of Syria and Cilicia (Acts 15:41), "every church" in every place (1 Cor. 4:17; Acts 14:23), "the churches of God" (1 Cor. 11:16), "the churches of Christ" (Rom. 16:16), "all the churches of the saints" (1 Cor. 14:33), and "all the churches" (7:17) mentioned in the New Testament refer to local churches, which were many local expressions of the one universal church in the first century on this earth both in the Jewish world and in the Gentile world.

ONE CITY, ONE CHURCH

Regarding the local churches, three provinces of the ancient Roman Empire are mentioned in the New Testament: Asia, Galatia, and Macedonia. Because Asia, Galatia, and Macedonia were all provinces, the Bible mentions "the churches of Asia" (1 Cor. 16:19), "the churches of Galatia" (Gal. 1:2; 1 Cor. 16:1), and "the churches of Macedonia" (2 Cor. 8:1). There were many churches in one province because there were many cities in a province.

In one province you may have many churches, but in one city you should not have many churches. One city should only have one church, one local church. So Revelation 1:11 tells us that in the province of Asia there were at least seven local churches in seven cities. There was a church in the city of Ephesus, in the city of Smyrna, in the city of Pergamos, in the city of Thyatira, in the city of Sardis, in the city of Philadelphia, and in the city of Laodicea. In each one of these seven cities, there was one local church. In many cities there are many local churches, but in one city there must be only one local church. The local churches are the expressions of the one universal church. When we say the practical expression of the church, we mean the local churches.

TWO OR THREE MEETING TOGETHER

We are all aware of the confusion of the denominations and how wrong they are. There is no need to mention them. But I do have a burden to speak of the so-called free groups. I have read some books and heard many teachers say that wherever two or three are meeting together in the name of the Lord Jesus Christ, that is the church. This kind of writing and speaking, in a sense, encourages people to meet just by two or three, especially in today's confusion and differences of denominations. People see the evil influence of the denominations, so they decide to meet in their homes or other places based upon the principle of meeting by two or three.

The scriptural ground used by all those meeting by two or three is Matthew 18:20. But they actually misinterpret, misuse, and even usurp this verse. They say, "The Lord Jesus tells us that where two or three are meeting in His name, He will be in their midst. Is not this good enough? Is not this the church?" Some Christian teachers, based upon this verse, even insist that there is no need of the local church. They say that as long as two or three meet in the name of the Lord Jesus, it is the church. A number of people have been influenced by this kind of teaching. They simply do not care for the principle of one local church in one city. They think that as long as two or three meet in the name of the Lord, they also are the church. But if we read Matthew 18 carefully, we will see that two or three cannot be the church if there are more believers in one locality. It tells us clearly that if we have some problem which cannot be resolved with *two or three* believers, we must bring the problem to the church.

Let us read Matthew 18:15-20 again in order to have the Word accurately impressed upon us. Then we can never be led astray. "Moreover if your brother sins against you, go, reprove him between you and him alone. If he hears you, you have gained your brother. But if he does not hear you, take with you one or two more, that by the mouth of *two or three* witnesses every word may be established. And if he refuses to hear them, tell it to the church [The church is *another body,* including the two or three]; and if he refuses to hear the church also, let him be to you just like the Gentile and the tax collector. Truly I say to you, Whatever you bind on the earth shall have been bound in heaven, and whatever you loose on the earth shall have been loosed in heaven. Again, truly I say to you that if two of you are in harmony on earth concerning any matter for which they ask, it will be done for them from My Father who is in the heavens. For where there are two or three gathered into My name, there am I in their midst."

In these verses the Lord's word is very clear and definite that two or three meeting in His name are one thing, and the church is another; the two or three cannot be the church, but only a part of the church, if there is in their locality a church existing of more than two or three. Therefore, even if we meet in the name of the Lord by two or three, having the Lord in our midst, we still cannot be the church if our number of two or three does not include all the saints in our locality. To have the Lord's presence is one thing, but to be the church is another. This passage does not mean that to have the Lord's presence means that we are the church. We must all be definitely clear that this kind of teaching about two or three meeting in the name of the Lord to be the church is absolutely wrong! This kind of inaccurate teaching has opened and still opens the back doors for division and confusion. It encourages and justifies divisions. If we take this kind of back door, there will be no limitation to us and no lessons for us to learn. The local church—that is, only one church in one city—is a real restriction and a real limitation. But praise the Lord, this restriction is a kind of protection. When we are restricted, we are protected.

Do not accept this kind of teaching of two or three meeting together to be the church. It is really dangerous. If you take this teaching, a time will come when you will feel unhappy with those with whom you are meeting. You will look at Brother So-and-so and say that you simply do not like him. Of course, he is probably one of the leading ones in the meeting. As you look at the others, you will think that some are not so bad, but most of them you simply do not like. Later, you will speak with someone: "Brother, what do you feel about these people here?" He will probably have the same feeling. Then you two will come together to pray, seeking the Lord's mind. The more you pray, the more you are burdened that you must start another meeting in one of your homes, and you feel that this is of the Lord. You say, "We should not follow man; we have to follow the Spirit. Moreover, we have the scriptural ground in Matthew 18:20. The Lord is not so narrow. He is merciful. As long as we call upon Him, He will be good to us."

This is the real situation today. But we must be made clear by the Lord's Word that to meet in the Lord's name and have the Lord's presence and blessing in our midst is one thing, while the church is another. We should not confuse these two. Regardless of how good the Lord is to us, the one can never be the other.

You may love the Lord and help many people to be saved. Perhaps in the beginning you only had two or three, but in half a year you may have fifteen. Then in another six months you may have twenty-five or possibly more. But parents always produce children after their kind. So after about two years, two or three brothers among your new group will feel unhappy with you because you are now the leaders, and they will repeat your previous performance. They will consult and pray until they feel that they should form another meeting of two or three. They feel that they have the Lord's leading and the scriptural ground in Matthew 18:20. They will do exactly as you did.

In this way, the divisions will be endless. Yet all the groups are in the same city, and in some places the different meetings are not distant from one another. They are not only in one city but also in close proximity. All of them claim to be meeting in the name of the Lord and testify that they have the presence of the Lord. The Lord has really answered their prayers, they say, and they have brought a good number of people to the Lord. They will ask, "If we are wrong, how could the Lord answer our prayers and bless us?"

But if we take this way, there will be no lessons for us to learn. There will be no limitations and no restrictions—only many back doors and "fire escapes." Please listen to the clear word of the Lord. The church in the universe is one, and the expression of the church in any locality must also be uniquely one. There is no choice. If we mean business with the Lord for the Body life and the oneness of His Body, why must we be separated? Why do we not come together as one unique local expression of the church since we are all in the same city?

THE LESSONS OF THE LOCAL CHURCH

If I am in a certain city, regardless of how I feel about those who are meeting there as the unique local church and regardless of how they treat me, I have no choice. I have to learn the lesson of the cross. I must learn the lesson of brokenness and self-denial. I have no ground, no right, and no standing to start another church in that locality as long as a unique one is there already. I must be restricted and limited. This is the real lesson.

The first year I went to Shanghai was in 1933. At that

time there was a brother in the church who was exceedingly active. He invited me to his home, and we had some fellowship. For a short time I thought this brother was quite good, but not long after, I discovered that he was exceedingly ambitious to be one of the elders. But he was not the right person to be an elder, so he was not confirmed as one. Then he became a real problem to the church life because he was ambitious to be one of the elders. The church was very patient with him for fifteen years. But in 1948 he established a meeting in his home and turned his back upon the church.

Thus, we see that without the limitation of the unique local church, we are free to behave as we like, and there is no lesson for us to learn.

We must read Matthew 18:15-20 again and see not only the church but also the authority of the church. There is restriction and limitation. How I thank the Lord for His restriction and limitation through the church. Many times we wanted to do something, but because of the limitation and restriction of the church, we could not do as we pleased. We felt somewhat unhappy at the time, but later, when we looked back, we had to say, "Lord, how we thank You. That was a real protection and blessing to us." It was not only an outward blessing but also a subduing and reducing of the self. We all must be reduced and restricted.

By the Lord's wisdom and sovereignty, wherever there is a local church, that must be the unique expression of the Lord's Body in that city. If we are going to stay in that locality, we must be one with that church. Then we will learn the lessons, and there will be no divisions, back doors, or "fire escapes." Every side will be closed. We must be restricted. But praise the Lord, it is by these restrictions that we are protected. The expression of the church is the local churches, and a local church is always unique. It is this unique expression of the church in every locality that is a lesson and restriction to us as well as a protection.

We must not be confused by today's situation but simply come back to the pure light of the Bible. Christians today have not seen clearly and definitely that the expression of the church is the local churches. Some always consider that wherever and whenever Christians meet together, it is good enough. This kind of consideration has been much encouraged by many Christian teachers and writers. Many messages and books encourage people to meet freely in their homes, on the campus, in the factories, and in so many quarters. People simply do not have the concept of the local church as the unique expression of the Lord's Body in their locality.

We need to have our eyes opened, for if we have not seen the local church, we are in darkness and under a blindfold. We may think that we are right, but in reality we are entirely wrong. We need a clear vision of the Lord's way concerning the church—that is, the local church is the unique expression of the church in every locality. If we see this vision, all problems will be solved.

THE LORD'S TWOFOLD RECOVERY

The Lord's recovery is mainly twofold: the spirit and the local expression of the church. We must have these two sides, these two aspects. The aspect of the spirit is for life, and the aspect of the local church is for the way. We need the life within, and we need the way without—the Lord will recover both.

In the past forty years the Lord has shown the church the need for the expression of the Body. But we must point out that the expression of the Lord's Body is only in one unique way: the local church. Regardless of how much you talk about the expression of the Body and are for the expression of the Body, until you have a unique, proper, practical, and living local church in your locality, you can never have the proper expression of the Body.

Today we are in the recovery of the Lord. On one hand, the Lord has shown us that we must experience Him as the life-giving Spirit in our spirit all the time, and at the same time He has also directed us to come together as the proper expression of His Body on the unique ground of the locality where we live. This is the local church. It is so real, so practical, so living, yet so simple. We must not be influenced by the present situation of today's Christianity but come back to the pure word of the Lord.

In the training meetings at Los Angeles in 1965, the Lord impressed us with two little phrases which we have never forgotten: *in the spirit* and *on the ground*. The one must be our life, and the other must be our standing.

CHAPTER FOUR

THE PRACTICALITY OF THE CHURCH

In the last chapter two points were covered: (1) the real need of the local churches to be the expression of the church, and (2) two or three meeting together in the name of the Lord cannot be the church if there is already a church in that place.

I believe these two points have been made clear to us. Therefore, in this chapter we want to go on to see the practicality of the church. I do not mean the reality of the church, but the practicality of the church. The reality of the church is Christ. When we say the practicality of the church, we do not mean the spirituality of the church, for this also is Christ. The practicality of the church is something else which we need to see.

THE PRACTICALITY OF THE LOCAL CHURCH

Brother Watchman Nee once stayed in a certain place for some time. When he was about to leave, the people asked him to give a parting word. He spoke to them in this way: "There is much talk today about the church, the Body of Christ. It is just like a group of carpenters talking about making chairs. I have heard so many good speeches about making 'chairs,' but I would ask, where are the 'chairs'?" This word is so simple but so impressive and practical. "Where are the 'chairs'?"

There have been many teachings and writings concerning the church, the Body of Christ, over a period of many years. But where are the churches that have come out of these teachings and writings? There has been a long period of speaking about making "chairs," but it is difficult to find one "chair."

This is why we need to see the practicality of the church. What is the practicality of the church? It is the local church. Without the local church, the church is not practical; it is like something in the air. We may have much talk about the church but nothing practical. We need the local church. The practicality of the church is in the local church.

The local church is not only the expression of the church but also the practicality of the church. If we would practice the church life, we must have the local church.

A CHURCH TO WHICH WE CAN GO

In Matthew 16:18 the Lord says, "Upon this rock I will build My church." This is the universal church. But if we go on to 18:17, we see the local church. I know some Christian teachers who take a stand by using only Matthew 16:18. They ask, "Is the church mentioned in this verse the local church?" They seem to present a strong argument. We agree that in Matthew 16:18 it is not the local church, but we cannot drop Matthew 18:17. We must go on from Matthew 16 to Matthew 18. Is the church in Matthew 18 the local church or the universal church? If it is the universal church, the church in the heavens, how could we go to it today when we have a problem? Matthew 18 says that if we have a problem to be solved by the church, we must go to the church. If this church is not the local church but something in the heavens, how can we go to it today?

If in any locality there is not a local church, regardless of how much we talk about the church, we do not have the practicality. In the past years I have noticed how many Christian teachers have spoken and written so much about the church. But eventually they did not have its practicality. Where is the practical church on this earth? Where is it?

Matthew 16:18 is precious, but Matthew 18:17 is practical. A local church may not be as spiritual as it should be, but it is practical to us. The church in Los Angeles may not be as marvelous as that mentioned in Matthew 16:18, but we have it and we enjoy it. Hallelujah! It is a church to which I can go. I cannot go to the church mentioned in Matthew 16:18. It is so wonderful, but where is it?

Therefore, regardless of how poor and weak the church in Los Angeles may be, we do have a church here. It is better than something in the air. When we have a problem, we do have somewhere to go. This is something practical.

In fact, Matthew 16:18 is included in Matthew 18:17. If we have Matthew 18:17, we have Matthew 16:18. How could we have Matthew 16:18 without Matthew 18:17? We cannot have the church without the local church.

From Matthew 18 we go on to the following Gospels. Mark did not say anything about the church; neither did Luke or John. Then we come to the book of Acts. Is there a verse in Acts that tells us something about the universal church? All the verses in Acts regarding the church refer to the local churches. They are the church mentioned in Matthew 18, which, as we have said, includes the one mentioned in Matthew 16.

The first verse mentioning the church in Acts is 5:11. After the death of Ananias and Sapphira, fear came upon the whole church. Undoubtedly, this is the local church at Jerusalem. The second and third times that the word *church* is used are in 8:1 and 3: "The church which was in Jerusalem." The fourth mentioning is in 9:31: "Then the church throughout the whole of Judea and Galilee and Samaria had peace." All of these verses refer to local churches on the earth. The church mentioned in 11:22 is "the church which was in Jerusalem," and that mentioned in 11:26 is the church in Antioch. The church mentioned in 12:1 and 5 is again the church in Jerusalem. Then in 13:1 we see the local church in Antioch. In 14:23 Paul and Barnabas appointed elders in every church. These, of course, are the local churches. In Acts 14:27 it is the church in Antioch again. In 15:3-4 it was the church in Antioch that brought Paul and Barnabas on their way and the church in Jerusalem that received them. In 15:22 it is the church in Jerusalem again. In 15:41 there are the local churches of Syria and Cilicia. In 16:5 there are the churches of the Gentile world (see 15:23). In 18:22 again we have the church in Jerusalem. In 20:17 and 28 it is the church in Ephesus.

Are all these churches in Acts the church in the heavens? No, they are all the local churches on the earth.

After Acts come the Epistles. In all these books the local churches are mostly dealt with. Only somewhat more than ten verses, most of which are in Ephesians, deal with the universal church (1 Cor. 10:32; 12:28; Eph. 1:22; 3:10, 21; 5:23-25, 27, 29, 32; Col. 1:18-24). The book of Romans was written to the church in Rome. First and 2 Corinthians were written to the church in Corinth. Nearly all the Epistles were written to local churches.

After the Epistles we have the book of Revelation, which is the conclusion of the New Testament. It was written to the seven local churches in Asia (1:4, 11) and reveals that the Lord Jesus is in the midst of the local churches. He is walking in the midst of the seven golden lampstands, which are seven local churches (vv. 13, 20; 2:1). It also reveals to us that the ultimate consummation of the church is the New Jerusalem, which is in eternity (22:1-5). But in time, while we are on this earth today, we must be in the local churches. Without the local churches there is no practicality to us of the church. When the ultimate consummation comes, we will have the New Jerusalem. But before that day, all we have practically is the local church. *If we do not have the local church today, practically speaking, we do not have the church.* The local church is the practicality of the church. The church today is practically in the local churches.

FOUR ASPECTS
OF THE PRACTICALITY OF THE CHURCH

The Building

There are four main aspects regarding the practicality of the church. First of all, the practical building up of the church is in the local churches. Without the local churches, how could the church be built? Suppose we do not have local churches, but we plan to build up the church in the heavens. How could we do it? It is impossible. Without the local churches there is no practical building. If we are not built with others in the local churches, we have never been built up in the church. The practicality of the building of the church is in the local churches.

The Administration

Then there is the administration, or the government, of the church. In the church there is the need of the government. Even in Matthew 18 the government of the church is mentioned. If we have a problem with a brother which we cannot solve with two or three, we must bring it to the church. The church has government.

In the book of Acts and in all the Epistles, the government of the church is mainly centered in the elders. But without the local church, how could there be any elders? If two or three are the church, you will be an elder to yourself, and I will be one to myself. Everyone will be an elder. Then how could the elders be appointed?

In the first local church in Jerusalem, there were elders taking care of the government (Acts 11:30; 15:2, 4, 6, 22; 16:4; 21:18). Later, the apostle Paul appointed elders in every church (14:23). Thus, there were elders in the church in Ephesus (20:17). Afterward, Paul ordered Titus to appoint elders in every city (Titus 1:5)—not in every home but in every city. There should only be elders in a city according to the Scriptures. If just two or three meet in a home as the church, there is no need of having any elders in the city. But the local church in a city has the practical need of elders.

The administration, or government, of the church is in the local churches. If we do not have the local churches, we do not have this government. This is why so many prefer to say that two or three meeting together are the church. They do not want the government.

In the local church there is the government which is a real restriction and real test to our flesh and our natural self. If we know how independent our natural self is, we will be so willing to have the church. Then we will have a government to which we can submit. We all need to learn submission because of our independent self. This is why we need the government and restriction of the local church.

The book of 1 Peter also has something regarding the government of the church with the elders. Verse 1 of chapter 1 says, "Peter, an apostle of Jesus Christ, to the sojourners of the dispersion of Pontus, Galatia, Cappadocia, Asia, and Bithynia." Altogether, there are five provinces mentioned in this verse. Two of these five are very familiar to us, Galatia and Asia. Were there not churches in Galatia? Yes, for we have the book to the Galatians, which mentions the churches of Galatia (1:2), as well as 1 Corinthians 16:1. The book of Revelation also lists the seven local churches in Asia (1:4, 11). Therefore, according to the record of the Bible, there were many local churches in the provinces of Galatia and Asia.

Some have used 1 Peter 1:1 as ground to oppose the concept of the local church. The dissenting thought is that this is not a letter to the local churches, but to the sojourners dispersed throughout so many places, and since this is so, how could all these scattered ones be the living stones built up into one spiritual house (2:5) as a local church? This sounds reasonable, but 1 Peter is not only of two chapters. We must read on until we come to chapter 5. Verse 1 says, "The elders among you..." The elders among whom? It must be the elders among the scattered saints who were in the local churches. If the scattered saints were just the scattered ones without meeting with the local churches or just meeting by two or three, there would be no need of elders. According to the teaching of the New Testament, the elders among the Christians are in the local churches. If there were no local churches, there was no need of elders. If the scattered saints never met together, there was no need for them to have elders.

I do believe that Peter was writing to the scattered Hebrew Christians, yet they were in the local churches. They were scattered in Galatia, Asia, and other provinces, but they must have been in some local churches, since we have seen that there were many local churches both in Galatia and in Asia. We have a similar situation with the Chinese brothers and sisters scattered throughout America. If a brother in Taiwan wrote a letter to all the Chinese brothers and sisters in the U.S.A., this does not mean that there are no local churches in the U.S.A. In fact, most of them are in the local churches here in this country in which there are elders. The practical administration of the church with the elders is in the local churches.

The Work

Third, all the work of the apostles and prophets was practically in the local churches and for the local churches. Without the local churches it is rather difficult to have a practical work to edify the saints. The apostle Paul said, "I teach everywhere in every church" (1 Cor. 4:17). Without the local churches Paul simply did not have a place to work or teach. He taught in every church.

Without the local churches the Lord's work is impractical. Paul said that he directed the same thing in all the churches (7:17). In other words, without the local churches it is rather difficult for the apostles and the Lord's servants to do anything to fulfill the Lord's purpose. The practical work is in the local churches.

The Coordination

The last point is the coordination of the church. Without the local churches, how could we as members be practically coordinated together as a Body? If we would have the Body life, the church life, in a practical way, we must be coordinated with one another. Therefore, we need the local churches. Suppose the brothers in Los Angeles did not have the local church. How could they be coordinated? It would be impossible. You may talk, teach, and write very much about the coordination of the saints in the Body life, but without the local churches it is impractical.

We do praise the Lord that in these past few years, we have really experienced the practicality of the church life. We do have something practical with coordination and building together. We thank the Lord that there are local churches with a real submission and a good order. This is something practical, not just a teaching. We do have the practicality of the Body life in coordination. However, we are not satisfied. We are always pressing on.

To have a practical church life, we need the local churches. I would say one thousand times to all the brothers and sisters that you need a local church. Do you not agree that you need a local church? First Timothy 3:15 says that we need to know how to conduct ourselves in the house of God, which is the church of the living God. This could only be practical in a local church. I do believe the Lord is going to recover the real and practical church life to prepare His bride for His return.

YOU ALSO BEING BUILDED

In closing this chapter, we must read Ephesians 2:21-22: "In whom all the building, being fitted together, is growing into a holy temple in the Lord; in whom you also are being built together into a dwelling place of God in spirit." The apostle Paul added verse 22 as a kind of repetition. It seems that verse 21 is quite adequate: "In whom all the building, being fitted together, is growing into a holy temple in the Lord." Why does he need verse 22? "In whom you also are being built together into a dwelling place of God in spirit." What is mentioned in verse 21 is the so-called universal church, the whole Body of Christ. But Paul mentions the local church in verse 22. "You" refers to the saints of the local church in Ephesus. "You also are being built together into a dwelling place of God in spirit." Is the dwelling place of God in verse 22 different from the temple in the Lord in verse 21? No, the dwelling place of God in verse 22 is a part of the temple in the Lord in verse 21. One is local; the other is universal.

Bible teachers have always said that the book of Ephesians is not about the local church, but the universal church. They are right in that this book covers the universal aspect of the church, but it still deals with the local church. "In whom you also are being built together..." This is the building of the local church. Do not say that as long as we have the universal church it is good enough. Regardless of how much we have the universal church, we still need "In whom you also..."! We still need the local church, for without it, there is no practicality of the church.

CHAPTER FIVE

THE ONENESS OF THE CHURCH

Scripture Reading: Eph. 4:3-6, 13-16

For a proper and practical expression of the church, we need to know the oneness of the church. The proper local church and the proper practice of the church depend on how much we know the church, and oneness is the foundation and the test of the practicality of the church life. If we can pass the test of oneness, then we are proper and right in our church practice. Therefore, in order to have a proper and practical church life, we need to be very clear about the oneness of the church.

THE ONENESS OF THE SPIRIT

What is the oneness of the church? The fourth chapter of Ephesians makes us very clear. "Being diligent to keep the oneness of the Spirit in the uniting bond of peace: one Body and one Spirit, even as also you were called in one hope of your calling; one Lord, one faith, one baptism; one God and Father of all, who is over all and through all and in all" (vv. 3-6).

The oneness of the church is the oneness of the Spirit, which is comprised of the Triune God. Here in Ephesians 4 the seven "ones" are divided into three groups, and every group has one of the three persons of the Godhead. In the first group we see the Spirit, in the second the Lord, and in the third God the Father. In group one there is the Body, the Spirit, and the hope. Then with the second group we see the Lord, the faith, and the baptism. The last group contains God the Father. With the Spirit is the Body and the hope. With the Lord is the faith and baptism. Then there is God the Father of all, who is over all and through all and in all. The Godhead in three persons is our oneness, which is realized in the Spirit.

The oneness of the church is nothing but the Triune God, the very God in three persons dispensed into us for the forming of the Body. It is quite interesting to notice that in these three groups, the Spirit is mentioned as the first, the Lord as the second, and God the Father as the third. This order is according to the formation of the Body, not according to the order of the Godhead. According to the order of the persons of the Godhead, God the Father is first, then the Lord, and then the Spirit. But according to the formation of the Body in our experience, the Spirit is first, then the Lord, and then God the Father. This is because God the Father is the source, the Lord is the course, and the Spirit is the application. It is in and with the application of the Spirit that the Body comes into existence. Without the Spirit it is impossible to have the Body.

When we have the Spirit, we are led to the Lord. When we have the Lord, we have the source who is God the Father. This is the oneness of the church. It is nothing but the Triune God realized in the Spirit. Thus, the oneness of the church is the oneness of the Spirit. The Father is in the Son, the Son is in the Spirit, and the Spirit is now in the Body. They are now four-in-one: the Father, the Son, the Spirit, and the Body.

How is all of this possible? How can the Triune God be one with the Body? It is only by faith and baptism. It is by faith that we get into the Lord and by baptism that all our oldness is ended. Faith brings us into Christ, and baptism brings us out of Adam. This is why we must believe and be baptized. It is by believing and being baptized that we are translated out of Adam and into Christ. We were born in Adam; so we were in Adam. But we were transferred out of Adam into Christ by believing and being baptized.

When we believe, we believe *into* Christ, and when we are buried in baptism, this burial terminates all our old relations. It is by these two things that we are in Christ and Christ is in us. Now in Christ we are one with the Triune God with a hope before us. Everything is accomplished; we only look forward to the hope. The hope is our future, our destiny, and our destination; it is the coming Christ or the coming of Christ. Christ is our hope, the hope of glory (Col. 1:27). At His return we will be glorified with Him and brought into His glory (Phil. 3:21; 1 Cor. 2:7; 1 Pet. 5:10).

This is the oneness. We are all really one in this—not one real Christian differs. We are all alike in the seven "ones." This is our oneness, and this oneness is the oneness of the Spirit. The Spirit is the reality of this oneness.

THE ONENESS OF THE FAITH

This oneness is also the oneness of the faith, the oneness of that in which we all believe. It is the oneness of the faith by which we are saved. As in the Spirit we are one, so in the faith we are also one.

In Ephesians 4:13-14 we see two terms: *the oneness of the faith* and *wind of teaching,* which refers to doctrine. What is the difference between the faith and doctrine? The faith is composed of the things that save us if we believe in them, such as the person and the redemptive work of Christ. If we believe in these, we are saved. The faith is composed of these. These things are the faith, not the doctrine. Doctrines have nothing to do with our salvation.

Some say that their faith is in immersion. Others say that their faith is in sprinkling. But are immersion or sprinkling part of the faith? The faith is absolutely necessary for our salvation, but neither sprinkling nor immersion are so necessary. Some may be immersed who are saved, while others may be sprinkled who also are saved. So neither immersion nor sprinkling has anything to do with our salvation. This proves that neither immersion nor sprinkling is part of the faith. Neither immersion nor sprinkling are heresy; both are doctrines, but neither are a part of the faith.

The faith has something to do with our salvation. If we have it, we are saved; if we do not have it, we are lost. This is the faith. But what is doctrine? Doctrine may benefit us, but it has nothing to do with our salvation.

In today's Christianity there are many doctrines such as head covering, foot-washing, baptism by immersion, or sprinkling. There are many doctrines which are all from the Bible but not part of the faith. They are just doctrines, having nothing to do with our salvation. Whether we have our heads covered or not, whether we practice foot-washing or not, whether we are baptized by immersion or by sprinkling, as long as we keep the faith, we are saved.

I have heard many in the past quoting Jude 3: "Contend for the faith once for all delivered to the saints." Therefore, they say, we must contend for the faith. Some take baptism by immersion as a part of their faith; so they contend for it. But baptism by immersion and so many other doctrines are not part of the faith; they are just doctrines. The Bible tells us to contend for "the faith," not for any doctrine. We must contend for "the faith," the saving faith, not for any doctrine that has nothing to do with our salvation.

Suppose a brother in the faith insists upon sprinkling. What should our attitude be? We may feel that it is better to be immersed; but if he insists on sprinkling, we must let him do it. As long as we all have the faith in the Lord, it is sufficient. If you insist upon sprinkling, I am still one with you. Though I am not for sprinkling, I am still one with you in the faith and in the Body. I would not be divided from you in the faith and in the church by any doctrine.

We should not make any doctrine a part of the faith. If we do, we make ourselves a "church" of a certain doctrine and become a sect of that doctrine. If we insist on sprinkling or immersion and make it a part of our faith, we become a sprinkling "church" or an immersion "church." These are not genuine churches, but divisions. Whether we practice immersion or sprinkling has nothing to do with the faith. As long as we simply keep the faith and do not make any doctrine a part of our faith, we are one. In the faith we are one; by the doctrines we are divided.

WIND OF TEACHING OR DOCTRINE

We must be exceedingly clear regarding the difference between the faith and doctrine. The faith is uniquely one, but doctrine may vary. Thus, the faith unites, but doctrine may divide. With the faith there is surely oneness, but with doctrine there is the possibility of division. Any doctrine, regardless of how good it is, can be divisive. We should be alert not to allow any doctrine to divide us. "Be no longer little children...carried about by every wind of teaching." Any doctrine other than the faith, even the best doctrine, can be a "wind" carrying us away from taking Christ as our center and from the proper church life. If we are careless regarding the Lord's unique purpose concerning the church and do not give it our full attention, we may be carried away from the Lord's central purpose by the "wind" of some doctrine. We must hold Christ, cleave to His Body, and keep the oneness of the faith in the oneness of the Spirit. Never be carried away from the oneness of the faith by the wind of any doctrine. The oneness of the faith is first. We must stand for the oneness of the faith forever, not for any doctrine. Let no doctrine be a "wind" to us! We really need the Lord's deliverance and the Lord's protection.

THE NEED OF GROWTH IN LIFE

In order to keep the oneness of the faith and not be carried away by the wind of doctrine, we need the growth in life. If we remain in childhood, we may be easily carried away by the wind of some doctrine. The doctrines may be good, but they are simply toys. Toys are not wrong, but toys are for children. The younger you are, the more you enjoy toys. Do you still toy with doctrines? I can assure you that the more you grow in the Lord, the more you will drop the toys of doctrine.

Ephesians 4:14-15 tells us clearly what doctrine can do if we have not grown up into Christ in all things. As long as we are children, it is easy for the subtle enemy to deceive us by using certain doctrines to distract us from the proper church life, as a wind carrying us away from the proper course. Why? Because children like toys, and the doctrines are just like toys! The more we grow in life, the more we will drop the toys of doctrine.

Forty years ago, baptism by immersion was a real toy to me, and so were many other doctrines. But by His mercy I can hardly say what toy of doctrine I still have today. We must learn never to insist on any doctrine, but just upon the faith. Doctrines divide; only the faith unites.

We all need to be delivered from the toys of all kinds of doctrines. However, it must not be an outward deliverance but a deliverance issuing from the growth in life. We need to grow. While we are still growing, we must realize that we should not insist on any toy. As long as the saints believe in the Lord Jesus as the Son of God, incarnated to be a man, dying on the cross for our sins, resurrected, and ascended to the heavens, we must be one with them. If the Lord Jesus is our unique center, there will be no problem.

INSISTING ON NOTHING BUT THE FAITH

While I was visiting some places in this country, there were some who asked whether it was scriptural to be baptized more than once. I did not say a word. If we have grown in the Lord, we will not pay much attention to doctrinal things. All we will care for is the faith and the oneness.

Some people are offended by sisters having their head covered. That is in large measure a matter of opinion. As long as a sister feels that she must cover her head, there is no need to oppose it. But there are also some who impose head covering, making it a legalistic matter. This is the other extreme.

Some oppose pray-reading, and some condemn loud praising. All this is dissenting opinion and unnecessary. As long as people take the Word of God and praise the Lord, regardless of the way we prefer that they do it, we should not oppose them. If we do, we go too far. On the other hand, if we insist on these things and impose them upon others, we go too far in the other direction.

Since we have seen that the local church is the practical expression of the church, we should not insist on anything but the faith. If anyone says that the Lord Jesus is not the Son of God, we must contend for it. This is contending for the faith. But if a sister feels that she does not need to have her head covered, she should be left to act according to her own feeling in this matter. This is the church life, and this is keeping the oneness. Regarding matters of dissent, the apostle teaches in Romans 14:1-6 that we should take a very liberal attitude in receiving one another in order to keep the oneness of the Body.

WRECKED FOR THE LOCAL CHURCH

Now this matter of the oneness of the church is very clear to us. First of all, we should not insist on anything but the faith, and we should not impose anything other than the faith on others. Second, we should not be influenced by any kind of wind of teaching. We must "stick" to the local church. Regardless of what others teach, we should not be distracted. If we pay attention to any kind of doctrine, it will be exceedingly easy for us to be carried away by the wind of doctrine from the oneness of the Body. We must be for the local church—nothing else.

We must be just like the wood that is used to build a wooden stand. All the pieces of wood are good for nothing *but* the stand; they have been ruined for everything else. In the same way, we all need to be ruined for everything but the local church.

Some friends with good intentions have come to me and said, "Brother Lee, we love you, but you have taken the wrong way. If you would not take this way of the local church, but do as we do, you would be much in demand. We are so sorry for you." They are sorry for me, but I am so happy for myself. I like to be wrecked for the local church. I like to be ruined for the church life. I am good for nothing *but* the church life. I do not care about a certain kind of doctrine or a certain kind of spiritual teaching; I only care for the local church.

Praise the Lord! The goal is so clear to us, and the way is so certain to us. We have no other choice but the oneness. We must not care for anything but the oneness. There is one Body, one Spirit, and one hope. There is one Lord, one faith, and one baptism. There is one God and Father of all. Therefore, we are all one. This is why we are so broad and so all-inclusive. We do not care for anything but the faith.

ARRIVING AT THE ONENESS OF THE FAITH

May we have the Lord's grace that we may keep the oneness by the growth in life. We must grow and grow in life until we drop all the toys of different doctrines or teachings and "all arrive at the oneness of the faith" (Eph. 4:13).

At the time we were saved, we all had the oneness of the faith. But afterward, due to our childhood, we gradually picked up many different doctrines by which we were intentionally or unintentionally divided. If we grow in life, we will spontaneously and gradually drop the doctrines of dissent. The more we grow in the Lord, the more we will relinquish the doctrinal toys. The more mature we become, the less we will take pleasure in doctrines. One day, by the growth and maturity of life, we will "arrive at the oneness of the faith," and all the toys of doctrines which immature ones keep will disappear.

Oh, how we need to return to the oneness of the faith from so many doctrines or teachings of dissent! So many of us have been carried away by the "wind of doctrine" for too long a time. Now is the time for us to be brought back. This requires a real turn to the Lord and growth in life. For the church life we need to be brought back to the oneness of the faith. For the local church we need to be brought back from all the divisive doctrines of dissent. For the Lord's recovery of the genuine Body life, we need the genuine oneness, which is both the oneness of the Spirit and the oneness of the faith. All the divisive doctrines must go; only the Spirit and the faith should remain. May the Lord have mercy upon us and all His children.

CHAPTER SIX

THE GROUND OF THE CHURCH

Scripture Reading: Acts 14:23; Titus 1:5; 1 Cor. 1:10-13; 11:19; Gal. 5:20; Titus 3:10

In the past chapters we have seen the eternal purpose of God, the expression of Christ, the expression of the church, the practicality of the church, and the oneness of the church. After the oneness we must see the ground of the church.

THE MEANING OF THE GROUND OF THE CHURCH

First of all, we must see the meaning of the term *the ground of the church*. When we say the ground, we do not mean the foundation. I am afraid that many people confuse these two words. The ground of the church is not the foundation.

Suppose we have a piece of land upon which we wish to put a house. This lot, or site, is what we call the ground. The ground is the very site where the building is placed. It is upon this piece of land that the foundation is laid and the building is erected. Most every building has a foundation, and the main part of the foundation of most buildings is underneath the ground. So there is the ground, and there is the foundation. The ground is the site upon which the house is built, and the foundation is the base of the house. These are two separate things.

First Corinthians 3:9 tells us that Christ is the only foundation. This means that Christ is the base of the building of the church. He is the foundation upon which the church is built. But if Christ is only the foundation, what is the ground? The ground must be the very place where we build the church with Christ as the foundation.

Suppose I place a vase upon a table. Then the table becomes the ground to hold the vase. But if I hold the vase in the air, it does not have a ground. If I put the vase upon a brother's head, his head becomes the ground. If I hold it in my hand, then my hand becomes the ground. But neither his head nor my hand is the proper ground. The vase must be on the table; then it is on the proper ground, the place where it belongs.

It is possible to have the right thing on the wrong ground. It is something right but on the wrong ground. We must have the right thing, but we must also have the right thing on the right ground.

JERUSALEM—
THE GROUND OF THE TEMPLE

We know that in Jerusalem a temple was built according to the design revealed by God and with all the materials designated by God. Therefore, Jerusalem was the ground of the temple. Then one day the people of Israel were carried away to Egypt, Syria, and Babylon. Suppose they built a temple in the same design and with the same materials in these three places. The temple would be right, but it would be on the wrong ground. Then there would be four temples in the same design, with the same materials, and even with the same measurements. It would seem as if they were all right. But each would have a different ground. The three temples outside of Jerusalem would be the same as that in Jerusalem, but they would be on the wrong ground.

Now suppose the temple in Jerusalem, which was the one on the proper and unique ground, was destroyed, and the one built in its place in the recovery was somewhat smaller; it was not exactly the same as the original. But in Babylon a big temple was built exactly the same as the original one in Jerusalem. In other words, in Babylon there was a temple up to standard, but in Jerusalem the temple was below standard. In this kind of situation, to which temple should we go?

When we read Ezra and Nehemiah, we see the poor condition existing among those who returned to Jerusalem. Some of them even took heathen wives. There was very little spirituality among them. But Daniel was in Babylon, and he was a spiritual giant. Why should anyone go to Jerusalem to be with those poor, pitiful ones who took heathen wives? It seems that it would be much better to stay in Babylon with Daniel.

What would you do? Would you stay in Babylon with the spiritual prophet Daniel, or would you go back to Jerusalem with those poor ones? We all need clear discernment in this matter. There was real spirituality with Daniel, but Daniel was not in Babylon for Babylon. He opened his window toward Jerusalem and prayed three times a day (Dan. 6:10). He was so desirous to go back, but under God's sovereignty he had to stay. He had to stay not for Babylon but for Jerusalem.

We also know that God's glory was not in Babylon. His presence, in a sense, was there with some person or persons, but His glory was not there. It was not until the destroyed temple was rebuilt in Jerusalem, even though it was not up to standard, that the glory of God filled it (Hag. 2:7, 9). The glory was not in Babylon but in Jerusalem with a poor group of people. This was entirely due to the ground.

Do you think that the temple being rebuilt on the proper ground and the glory of God being manifested were due to the spiritual situation? Had the people's condition changed? No, it had not changed. It was still the same. But because a building was erected on the proper ground, even though it was under the standard, the shekinah glory of God was manifested. This was not because the spirituality of the people had been greatly improved. That did not bring in God's glory. It was simply due to the fact that they came back and rebuilt the temple on the proper ground. Though their situation and condition were poor, their standing and their ground were right. God honored the ground they took and upon which they built.

It was only a little over four hundred years following the return of the captives that the Lord Jesus was born. Was He born with the group that stayed with Daniel? No, the Lord Jesus was born to the poor returned group in Israel. When we read the four Gospels, we see how poor and pitiful the state of the Lord's people was in Israel when the Lord was born.

But the Lord Jesus came to this earth the first time through them because they were on the right ground.

Suppose that not one of the scattered Israelites had returned to Jerusalem. Instead, they all remained in Babylon, with some in Syria and Egypt. If so, could the Lord Jesus be born in the land of Israel? No, He could not come because the ground would not be available.

THE GROUND OF THE CHURCH

Now let me ask, What is the ground of the church? In principle we have seen the meaning of the ground and its importance, but we must apply it. What is the ground of the church? The ground of a certain thing is the very place where you put that thing. That is the ground. In other words, the ground of the church is the very place where the church is.

If a vase rests on a table, the ground of the vase is the table. Then what is the ground upon which the church stands? It is the city where the church is. The first church in the New Testament was in Jerusalem (Acts 8:1). It is very clear that the city of Jerusalem became the ground of that church.

Then the church spread from Jerusalem to Antioch. Since there was now a church at Antioch (13:1), spontaneously the city of Antioch became the ground of the church there. Then the church spread from Antioch to Ephesus, Corinth, and many other cities. All the cities where the church spread became the ground upon which the church stood. This is the unique ground of the genuine oneness. This is the local ground, or the ground of locality.

Suppose that in Corinth some of the believers who liked Apollos were to build an Apollonian church, and those of Peter were to build a Petrine church. Then there would be a church of Apollos and a church of Peter. Then suppose those of Paul were to build up a Pauline church, and even some would say that they were of Christ, so they would build up a "church of Christ." Then, there would be four churches in the one city of Corinth, and all of these four churches would claim, declare, and proclaim that Christ is their foundation. The Apollonian church is built on Christ, the Petrine church is built on Christ, the Pauline church is built on Christ, and, of course, the "church of Christ" is also built on Christ. All four different kinds of churches claim to have Christ as their foundation. Their foundation may be the same, but their grounds are absolutely different. They are all built on different grounds. One has the Apollonian ground, one has the Petrine ground, one has the Pauline ground, and one even says that Christ is its ground. What are these grounds? We must be clear that they are all divisive. Only Corinth is the right ground. The ground of locality is the one unique and uniting ground upon which the church can be built. The unique, proper ground of the church is the locality where the church is.

Today we have the same thing in a city such as Los Angeles. There is a church built upon the Presbyterian ground, a church built upon the Baptist ground, a church built upon the Methodist ground, and so many kinds of "churches" built upon so many kinds of grounds. In one city there are many kinds of "churches" because they are on so many different kinds of grounds. All of these grounds are divisive.

We must be clear that the ground of the church is the very locality where the church is. When we go to Jerusalem, we must go to the church in Jerusalem. When we go to Antioch, we must go to the church in Antioch. Then the divisions are gone. When we go to a certain city, we must go to the church in that city.

But the big problem is this: Suppose I like sprinkling, and the church in the city where I go practices immersion. What should I do? The usual thing that happens is that I will talk with the saints there, argue with them, and eventually start a new "church" that practices sprinkling. Then upon what is my "church" built? It is unquestionably built upon the ground of sprinkling. I have built it upon something which I believe is right, but it is built upon the wrong ground. It is not built upon the ground of locality, but on the ground of sprinkling.

Then someone else who practices speaking in tongues goes to the same city. But the church in that city does not practice tongues either. So eventually he does the same thing and builds a "tongue-speaking church." The ground of his "church" is speaking in tongues. But tongues should not be the ground upon which a church is built. It must be built upon the ground of locality. This is today's pitiful situation. Perhaps someone else also goes to the same place to build up a "church" of head covering. So there is another division. The tongue should not be the ground of the church; neither should head covering.

HOLDING THE GROUND AND MINISTERING CHRIST

I believe we can see all the different grounds of divisions. This is why we must give up all of these things. When we go to a place, as long as the church there is on the proper ground, we must be one with her. She may be weak, and she may need much improvement, yet she is still the church on the proper ground. If we go there, we must meet with her. We have no right and no standing to establish another thing. Whether she sprinkles or not, whether she practices speaking in tongues or not, whether she has head covering or not, we still must go along with her, because she is the church on the proper ground.

We must not hold to any doctrine, but simply cleave to the abundance of Christ's life. Regardless of what the church in a certain place practices, we must simply minister Christ to her. We must not care for the doctrines, but only for the rich supply of Christ to be ministered to her.

Perhaps the saints there would not even take pray-reading. Still we must minister Christ to them. Since they do not like pray-reading, we had better not speak with them about it, but be so strong in our spirit. Whenever we open our mouth in the meetings, the whole church will be subdued. We will pray, we will testify, and we will contact the saints in a living way. There is no need to fight for anything. As long as there is a church on the proper ground, we must be built up with her. She may not be so spiritual, but we do not care for that. We must only be on fire and burning in the spirit. Then we will burn others.

We must be so full of life—that is all. We must not bring anything to any place, and we must not stand for anything but Christ and the church on the proper ground. If we are full of Christ and so strong in the spirit, nothing can stop us from burning others. Eventually, the whole church in that place will be burnt by us.

We must learn to keep the ground and not to stand for anything else. As long as there is nothing sinful in the church where we are, we must go along with her. Then we should simply minister Christ to the people. We must never cause division, but always minister Christ.

We really need to be delivered from all our doctrines. We must be for nothing but Christ and the church. As long as the church is on the proper ground, regardless of how poor and weak she is, we must be one with her. Then we will never be divisive.

Some may say that the principle of one church in one city is right, but it is not applicable today. Today it is impossible, they may say, for all the saints in one locality to come together as one church. But regardless of the confusion, we must still keep and apply the principle. The majority of Christians will not take the proper ground, but the Lord will still raise up a remnant to stand on the ground of oneness. Whatever the Lord has ordained can never be abandoned. Regardless of all the failure in the past and in the present, the Lord will still accomplish it. It may be on a smaller scale, but the principle is still the same.

We do believe that in these last days the Lord will work out the local church on a smaller scale. Some seeking ones will be brought together to take the ground of oneness and testify thereon to the whole universe that they are one in Christ, regardless of their varying backgrounds. This will be a real glory to the Lord and shame to the enemy.

CHAPTER SEVEN

THE GENERAL ATTITUDE FOR ONENESS

Scripture Reading: Rom. 14:1-6; 15:7

TODAY'S PROBLEM

The problems prevailing today in Christianity are mostly due to our different opinions regarding certain things, and these different opinions are due to a shortage of Christ. We all have our own tastes and our own concepts in so many matters; but if we are in our opinions and our concepts, we only cause trouble. For instance, regarding the matter of baptism, there are many different opinions, and they have caused much trouble. However, if we are full of Christ, we will not care for these things.

THE APOSTLE'S ATTITUDE

The attitude of the apostle Paul in Romans 14 regarding different concepts of eating and the keeping of days was exceedingly liberal and general. According to the teaching of the Bible, it is abundantly clear that today under God's grace, there is no need to make distinctions regarding the things we eat. All things are good for food, both meat and herbs—there is no difference in the eyes of God. We can eat herbs, and we can eat any kind of meat. The apostle Paul knew this better than we. But in this chapter he said not a word according to the doctrine regarding this matter. Instead, he said, "He who eats, let him not despise him who does not eat; and he who does not eat, let him not judge him who eats" (v. 3). If you eat all things, do not despise those who do not; if you do not eat all things, do not criticize those who do. What a liberal attitude the apostle tells us that we should take! As to the doctrine, he said not a word.

Concerning the keeping of days, the apostle said, "One judges one day above another; another judges every day alike. Let each be fully persuaded in his own mind." Again the apostle took a very liberal attitude, not saying which was right or which was wrong. According to the Scriptures, we should not keep any day in this age. Today, under the Lord's grace, every day is the same. Even the Sabbath differs not from any other day. The apostle knew this quite well, but he did not speak concerning the right doctrine. He did not say whether esteeming one day above another is right, or whether esteeming every day alike is right. He only said, "He who regards the day, regards it to the Lord" (v. 6). His attitude was truly liberal.

Could we be so liberal? We must be so liberal. By the Lord's mercy and grace, we must learn to be so liberal. I do not mean that we should be liberal regarding the Lord. We must be absolutely definite concerning the Lord and the church as His expression. But could we be liberal with all other things? Whether or not a brother or sister should do a certain thing depends upon his or her feeling before the Lord. If they feel they should do it, let them do it unto the Lord. Perhaps they will feel that they need not do it. Then let them not do it unto the Lord. If the Lord wants them to do it, they should not say no to Him.

We should not have any legal regulations, and we should not attempt to make everyone alike. If we insist upon having certain things in uniformity, we are legal. If one eats herbs and feels that everyone should also eat herbs, it will cause trouble. As long as the brothers and sisters do not do things that are sinful, we should not trouble them. We should only be definite regarding Christ as life and the church as the expression of Christ. With all other things, we must learn from the apostle Paul to be very liberal and general.

INSISTING ON NOTHING
BUT CHRIST AND THE CHURCH

We should not insist on anything, but keep the oneness for the church life in spite of all dissenting matters. We must be delivered from the divisive elements of all different opinions. How can we be delivered? It is only possible by caring only for Christ and the church. We must be filled with Christ and strong in our spirit for the church life.

Suppose I am a brother who loves to practice a certain thing which to me is very scriptural, and when I come to a certain local church, I find that the church opposes that very thing. But regardless how much they oppose it, they are still the church there. I am for that thing, because it helps me enjoy Christ; but since the church opposes it, I should not insist on practicing it in the public meetings. When I am at home, however, I will still practice it very much. Then I will be so burning with Christ that when I come to the meetings, I will come burnt and burning. I will not speak of that very thing, but I will be burning with Christ. If there is the slightest opportunity, the fire of Christ will get into the meeting through me. Whoever I contact, whether he be an elder or a brother, will be burnt. Perhaps after a certain time, the entire church will be burned by me.

We should not be for anything but Christ and the church. If I am one who is so much for doctrines and teachings, it is certain that I will cause trouble in the church. When I come to a certain local church and feel that they do not have any order, I will move to correct them. But if I do this, it proves that I do not know Christ so well as life and that I am not strong in the spirit for the church life. If I am full of Christ and strong for the church, I will not care what they do or what kind of doctrine they have; I will only praise the Lord that here is a local church on the proper ground where I can minister Christ. I will be afire in the spirit and so full of Christ that when I come to the meetings, I will minister Christ to others. I will be for Christ and the church—nothing else. I will not care for right things or wrong things; I will only care for Christ and the church.

If I am such a person, most of the seeking ones sooner or later will be helped by me, and the Christ whom I experience and minister will also be a living experience to them. This will keep the oneness and strengthen the church life. It is by keeping the oneness of Christ that the church is enriched; it is doctrines or different opinions that damage the Body. Eventually, the people in that place will not care for anything other than Christ and the church. They will not care for what is right or wrong; they will just care for Christ and the church.

THE WAY TO KEEP THE ONENESS

Here is the way for us to keep the proper oneness. We must not try to convince others of our opinions, but just be strong in the spirit, rich in the experience of Christ, and care for the proper church life.

There are always two things that cause problems in the church. The first is that people continually desire that others be the same as they. The second is that people want regulations. They always ask, "Which way is right? Is this the right way?" We are all like this, and we must by all means be delivered from these things. What we need is not regulations but to be filled with Christ and rich in the church life. We should not be for this way or for that way but just for Christ and the church.

In everything other than Christ and the church, we must be liberal and general. There is no need for us either to oppose or impose anything other than the Lord as life and the church as His expression. Perhaps some will think that I am too liberal and do not care for the Bible. But I would ask them to read Romans 14 again and care for this chapter as they care for the whole Bible. The apostle Paul is so liberal and general in this chapter, and he tells us to be such. The book of Romans has not only chapter 12 but also chapter 14. People today pay much attention to chapter 12 but neglect chapter 14. But without chapter 14, it is impossible to have the real Body life of chapter 12. The Body life of chapter 12 requires the liberal and general attitude of chapter 14 so that its oneness may be kept. Otherwise, it will be damaged by dissenting opinions and different concepts in certain matters. If we do mean that we care for the Bible, we must care for this chapter, Romans 14.

Perhaps there are some who do not like to hear everyone saying Amen in the meetings. But those who say Amen do have the ground to say it. When the people of Israel came into the land of Canaan, the entire congregation said Amen (Deut. 27:11-26), and in Revelation 5:14 and 19:4 the four living creatures and the twenty-four elders said Amen. They will turn to you and ask, "Where is your ground for not saying Amen?" Who is right and who is wrong? In any case, we must be liberal with all things like this. We must not care for all such things, but only for Christ and the church life.

I have a deep conviction that in these last days the Lord will recover the proper church life. He will not care for these doctrinal things, just as He did not care for such things when He first came. At that time the Lord Jesus and His forerunner, John the Baptist, abandoned all the religious customs. They did not surrender God, but they gave up the religion of Judaism. I believe that now, at the time of His second coming, the Lord will repudiate all the forms, regulations, and dead doctrines of Christianity.

THE PROPER WAY FOR THE CHURCH LIFE

The proper way to have the church life is simply to have Christ as the foundation upon the proper ground of oneness. That is all. We must not care for anything but Christ and His church on the proper ground of oneness. If we are strong in the spirit and full of Christ, it will be easy for us to go on with the local church, caring not for other things. Whether or not people play the piano in their meetings, we simply do not care. We only care to minister Christ to people and have the proper church life. We would not criticize or be occupied with different opinions. Whether people have the Lord's table in the morning or in the evening, it simply does not matter. As long as the church in our city is on the proper ground of oneness, we will be one with it and minister Christ in it. That is sufficient. We will relinquish all opinions and care not for any regulations. Then it will be exceedingly easy for us to go on with any local church with the ministry of Christ.

When Christians come to a new place, they always pay attention to the little things. Some always look to see whether the bread at the Lord's table is leavened or unleavened. Others want to know whether wine or grape juice is used in the cup. They always consider these trivial matters.

There are others who have certain kinds of rules and regulations for the Lord's table. These, of course, are not written but nevertheless understood. When they go to another place, they will be very critical if people do not practice the Lord's table as they do.

Oh, we all need the Lord's deliverance! We must see that we are not for these things. We are for Christ and His church. As long as the saints love the Lord and come together on the proper ground of oneness to minister Christ to one another, that is sufficient. We all must be fully occupied with Christ and the church on the proper ground. We must not pay attention to anything else. We must give others the freedom to act according to the way they feel led of the Lord. We must not criticize anyone according to our concept. All we need is to keep the oneness and minister Christ to people. We must be liberal in our attitude and strong in spirit.

As far as my realization is concerned, I do not like to use many small cups at the Lord's table. To me it is contrary to Scripture. I do not prefer baptism by sprinkling over baptism by immersion. To me, this also is unscriptural. I also feel that the sisters should cover their heads. But in all these past years I have never insisted upon these things, and I have never been troubled by them. When I go to a certain place, if the people use one large cup or many small cups, I will not be bothered. If you let me do it, I will have one large cup; but if you do it, you may have the liberty to do as you feel led of the Lord.

Wherever we go, wherever we are, we must go along with the church there. Perhaps we would like to practice immersion, but the church practices sprinkling. Then we should not impose immersion upon them. Of course, this does not mean that we should not fellowship with them regarding this matter. If they would take what we have seen, it is good; but if not, we should not cause trouble. If we realize that by speaking of a certain matter we will cause a disturbance, we should not say anything. Though we may not agree with them in certain things, we should not impose anything upon them or insist upon anything. We must go along with them in their way. If we are in a position to make a decision regarding certain things, perhaps we would not proceed in the same way. But if we are not in such a position, we should not say anything to create trouble. This does not mean that we agree with them in their way, but simply that we do not care for these things. We only care for Christ and the church. There is no other way for us to keep the oneness on the proper ground. We all must be so liberal; otherwise, sooner or later, we will create another division.

We must learn to be liberal and general. For anyone not to pray-read the Word, in my estimation, is a great loss. Whenever I open the Bible, I would pray-read. But if you do not do this, I am not troubled. Regarding things like this, we must have a general attitude. For the ground of oneness, we must be definite; but for other things, we must be general. Then we will have real oneness and a proper expression of the Body of Christ in the city where we live. This is the proper and unique way to practice the church life.

THE PROPER RECEIVING OF THE SAINTS

It is only by being so liberal and general that we can receive all the saints in the proper way. If we are otherwise, we cannot avoid being sectarian in the matter of receiving. If we are special in anything and insist upon that, we will probably not receive those who differ from us in certain matters. But the apostle said, "Him who is weak in faith receive, but not for the purpose of passing judgment on his considerations" (Rom. 14:1). What he meant when he referred to "him who is weak in faith" is illustrated in the following verses, which cover the matters of eating and the keeping of days. By this we are affirmatively told that we must receive the saints who differ from us in these things. Any saint who holds a different opinion or concept regarding the things of which we are in favor, we must receive, "for God has received him." As long as he is a saint, as long as he has been received by God, we must receive him. Since God has received him, we have no right to reject him. Our receiving must be the same as God's receiving, no less and no more. God's receiving is the basis of our receiving. Our receiving must not be according to our taste, our opinion, or our assertion. It must be in accordance with God's receiving. It must be based upon God's receiving—nothing else.

God receives people according to His Son. As long as a person receives His Son, our Lord Jesus Christ, as his personal Savior, regardless of the concepts he holds regarding all other things, God receives him immediately. Since God receives people in this way, we too must receive people in the same way. Our receiving must be in accordance with God's receiving. If our receiving differs from His, it means that we are wrong: either we are more narrow or more broad than God. This will cause much trouble and damage to the church life.

God's receiving is based upon Christ's receiving, and Christ's receiving is in accordance with our faith in Him. Whoever believes in Him, He will receive. Whoever receives Him, He will never reject. He said, "Him who comes to Me I shall by no means cast out" (John 6:37). Since coming to Him, believing in Him, receiving Him, is the only condition for Christ's receiving, we must receive people upon the same basis with nothing added. As long as one believes in Christ our Lord, as long as he receives Him as his personal Savior, we must receive him with nothing else required. Regardless of how he may dissent in so many other things, as long as he is a real believer in the Lord, we have no choice but to receive him, for the Lord has received him. This is why the apostle said, "Therefore receive one another, as Christ also received you to the glory of God" (Rom. 15:1). We must receive whoever Christ has received. We must have such a proper receiving of all the saints so that we may keep the proper oneness; otherwise, we can never keep ourselves from being sectarian and causing much confusion and damage to the church life. To practice the church life by keeping the proper oneness, such a general receiving is necessary. May the Lord have mercy upon us.

CHAPTER EIGHT

THE GROUND OF LOCALITY

Scripture Reading: Acts 14:23; Titus 1:5; Rev. 1:11

THE CHURCH EQUAL TO THE CITY

Acts 14:23 says that elders are ordained in every *church,* but Titus 1:5 says that elders are ordained in every *city.* This means that "in every city" is "in every church," and "in every church" is equivalent to "in every city." To ordain elders in every church is not to ordain elders in every home or in any other kind of place, but in every city.

Then Revelation 1:11 says, "What you see write in a scroll and send it to the seven churches: to Ephesus and to Smyrna and to Pergamos and to Thyatira and to Sardis and to Philadelphia and to Laodicea." Have you noticed all the *to*s in this verse? The Lord tells John to write in a scroll and send it to the seven churches. Following this, he says, "To Ephesus and to Smyrna and to Pergamos and to Thyatira and to Sardis and to Philadelphia and to Laodicea." *To* is repeated seven times. Therefore, to the seven churches is to the seven cities, and to the seven cities is to the seven churches.

To my realization the use of so many *to*s in this verse makes the composition rather awkward. There must be a reason for this repetition. "Write in a scroll and send it to the seven churches." Then it says "to" the first place and "to" the second place and "to" the third place and "to" the fourth place and "to" the fifth place and "to" the sixth place and "to" the seventh place. Why did the Lord speak in this way? If it were written by me, I would simply say, Send it to the seven churches which are in Ephesus, Smyrna, Pergamos, Thyatira, Sardis, Philadelphia, and Laodicea. I would not use so many *to*s.

I do not believe that anyone would write this verse as it is. Every one of us would probably put all seven names after one "to." But the Lord did not do it in this way. He told John to send this book to the seven churches. Then He said to send it to this city and to that city. This clearly shows us that one church equals one city and represents that city.

When something was written and sent to the church in Ephesus, it was sent to the city of Ephesus, because the church in Ephesus represented that city in the eyes of the Lord. If we read Revelation 1:11 again, we will realize that this is what it means. This verse tells us clearly and definitely that a church in a place must be equal to the city in which the church is located, and it corresponds with Acts 14:23 and Titus 1:5. In these two verses we see that to ordain elders in every church is to ordain elders in every city, and to ordain elders in every city means to ordain elders in every church. This makes it abundantly clear that the sphere and limit of the church must be exactly the same as that of the city. In other words, the boundary, the jurisdiction, of the church is identical to that of the city.

We must believe that the wording used by the Lord in writing the Scriptures is exceedingly meaningful. Why would Acts 14:23 say to ordain elders in every church and then Titus 1:5 say to ordain elders in every city? Has the church something to do with the city? In a sense, the church has nothing to do with the city; but in the Lord's way, the boundary, the jurisdiction, of a local church must be the same as the city. Then in Revelation 1:11 the Lord Jesus makes it extremely clear that a local church is equal to the city in which it is located.

THE SHORTAGE OF THE BRETHREN

Before 1828, the year in which the Brethren were raised up, the concept of the church being local had not been seen clearly by Christianity. But after 1828 the Brethren, under the leadership of John Nelson Darby, began to see that the church must be local. Thus, the Brethren began to have their local assemblies, and the term *local assembly,* or *local church* began to be used. But they were not clear regarding the limit, or the boundary, of the local church. Eventually, the Brethren, especially the so-called Open Brethren, had many local assemblies in one city. Six years ago in a certain city, I met one of their responsible brothers, who told me that there were four Brethren assemblies in that one city, and these four assemblies had nothing to do with each other. Everyone was a separate, independent assembly with a different administration. In other cities, they have even more assemblies. They have been too free. When some brothers in their assemblies have felt unhappy with others, they have left and started another meeting. Yet they would say that they were not divided from the others but were still one in the Lord. Some met on one street and others met on another street, but both claimed to meet in the name of the Lord. Thus, they were not assemblies of the cities but assemblies of the streets. They had responsible brothers not in every city but on certain streets. This was and still is due to the fact that the Brethren have never seen the limit, or the boundary, of the local church.

THE VISION OF THE GROUND OF LOCALITY

Beginning in 1922 many local gatherings were raised up by the Lord in China. By 1933 Brother Watchman Nee, realizing the confusion among the Brethren assemblies and being greatly concerned regarding the boundary, or limit, of a local church, read through the New Testament again in order to be clear concerning this matter. By so doing, he came to see that the boundary of a local church is the boundary of the city in which the church is located. That was a real deliverance to us. We became very clear that the church in Shanghai covered everything within the city limits of Shanghai.

From 1934 Brother Nee became more and more clear, not only concerning the boundary of the local church but also concerning the ground of the local church. Then in 1937 he delivered a number of messages to us regarding this matter, which are now contained in the book entitled *The Normal Christian Church Life*. The most emphasized point in these messages is the local ground of the church. From the boundary of the local church, Brother Nee went on to see the ground of the local church. It was by 1937 that this became clear to us all, and it was at this time that the term *the ground of the church* was first used. Not only is the city limit the boundary of the local church, but the city itself is the ground of the church. The ground of the church is the city in which the church stands. If a vase stands on a table, the table is the ground upon which the vase stands. A local church stands in a city, so the city in which it stands becomes its very ground.

Since then, the Bible, and especially the New Testament, has been opened to us in this matter. From that time until now, there has been no further improvement in this simply because it cannot be improved upon. It is exceedingly clear that the church ground is the city, the very locality in which the church stands.

Some say that we have learned concerning the local church ground from the Brethren. But the Brethren did not see this. If they had seen the unique ground of the church, they could not have many assemblies in one city.

THE IMPORTANCE OF THE GROUND

Why is the church ground important and necessary, and why do we stress this matter so much? We must all realize that the church in the entire universe is one Body; thus, regarding the church, there is a real oneness. The church should not be divided. How could your body be divided? You can divide anything else, but you can never divide your body. As the Body of Christ, the church must be one.

This oneness of the church is expressed in many localities. It was expressed in Jerusalem, it was expressed in Antioch, and it was expressed in Corinth. But the many local expressions of the church do not mean that the church is divided. There is only one United States of America. But the United States has many expressions. In Toronto the United States has one consulate, or one expression; likewise, in Vancouver there is one, in Mexico City one, in Hong Kong one, in London one, in Tokyo one, and in Paris one. There are many expressions but only one United States. The many consulates of the United States throughout the world as her many expressions do not mean that she is divided. But there can never be more than one consulate of the United States in any one city. If in London today there were two consulates of the United States, it would mean that the United States is divided. Regardless of the size of a city, as long as a consulate of the United States is there, that consulate must be uniquely one. It may have many offices, but it must only be one consulate. Tokyo is the largest city on earth today, but it has only one American consulate. If there were more than one, it would mean division.

The church is one; she should not be divided. But the church must be expressed in many places. Therefore, in every city, if there is an expression of the church, that expression must be uniquely one. If it is otherwise, there is division, and that cannot be.

As an American citizen in Tokyo, would you need to choose to which American consulate you should go? Of course not; you have no choice in the matter, for there is only one American consulate in Tokyo. All you need to know is the address and how to get there.

The church today has been divided simply by many different kinds of expressions in one locality. After the Second World War, Christians became so free, especially in this country. They were dissatisfied with the denominations; so they left and formed many smaller groups. Formerly, the number of different kinds of expressions of the church was smaller, but now it has been greatly increased. I was told that in Southern California alone there are at least one thousand small Christian groups. Those who are in these smaller groups do not sense that they are divisive. They claim to be groups which are seeking the true way, but in fact they are many small divisions.

So many know that the large denominations are divisive and sectarian, but they simply do not realize the divisiveness of the small groups. If you point this out to them, they will say that they are all one in Christ. This sounds good, but it is just a kind of saying; in fact, they are not one, but divisive.

Suppose the United States were divided into three separate countries. What weakness would result! This is just the subtlety of the enemy with the church. He has divided the

Body of Christ not only into parts but into many pieces. This is why the church today is so weak.

THE GROUND NOT DEPENDENT ON THE CONDITION

Another problem regarding divisions concerns those who only care for spirituality. If the meetings of the local church are not so spiritual, they will not go along. They will separate themselves to meet in a more spiritual way. They do not care for the unique ground of the church. It may be that they are not clear that the ground of the church does not depend upon the condition of the church. The condition may fluctuate, but the ground, the standing, never changes. Today we may be very spiritual, but after two months we may not be so spiritual; and after two years, we may be worse. But if today we are weak, can you say that after two years we will not be strong? This, however, is a matter of condition, which easily fluctuates; but the standing of the ground can never change.

Suppose we have a family called the Smiths. Their standing as the Smith family is something which can never be altered. But the condition of the Smith family may be good today and bad tomorrow. However, the members of the Smith family stay together as a family because they are one family. As one family, regardless of how good or bad it is, it is still the Smith family. This is their standing, their ground.

Suppose one of the members of the Smith family thinks that his family is quite poor; so he goes to another family, and that family is much better. But after two years that family becomes much poorer than the Smith family. Then what shall he do?

The problem today is that Christians have no standing, no ground. They only look at the spiritual condition. "This group is more spiritual. I would like to be with them." But after two years I may be very unhappy with them, so I go to another place. If I am such a person, this means that I have no standing, no ground. I am always seeking a place according to the spiritual condition.

The condition fluctuates, but the ground remains the same. Who can change the site of a building? The building may be poor today, but after a few months it may be greatly improved. In three months the building may change in its condition, but the site, the ground, is forever the same.

THE ONLY WAY TO KEEP THE ONENESS

It is only by the unique ground of locality that the church can be kept one. Without this ground she will be spontaneously divided. The church is one, so the expression of the church must also be one. Regardless of how big or how small a city may be, the church must be uniquely one in that city. We should never be divided. Wherever we are, we are one, and wherever we go, we are one. If I go to San Francisco, I must go to the church in San Francisco. If I go to London, I must go to the church in London. If I come to Los Angeles, I must come to the church in Los Angeles.

The church is the same in boundary as the city. How many churches should there be in San Francisco? There should be only one, because in every city the expression of the church must be uniquely one. If we go to San Francisco, we must find where the church is and go to it. It is very simple. It is just like going to Tokyo or London to find the American consulate. The American consulate is our consulate because we are citizens of America. We need not ask to which American consulate we must go. We need only ask as Americans citizens, "Where is my consulate?" It is the same when we as Christians go to San Francisco. As Christians we should ask, "Where is the church?" and go to it.

But in fact, sometimes it is not so. For instance, a brother finds the church in San Francisco and goes to the meeting. First he looks at the brothers and then at the sisters. Then he sees the way they have their meeting and attempts to discern how spiritual they are. After this, he returns home to consider the whole situation and eventually decides that he will not go there anymore. He stays home to pray: "Lord, You know that I love You, and You know my heart. O Lord, You know how much I seek after You, and You know the situation in that church. Lord, You know how I cannot go along with that kind of people." The more he prays, the more he is clear that he must start a meeting in his home, intending that it will be a more spiritual meeting than the church meeting he attended.

Thus, he begins to meet with others in his home with a very pure intention. They meet in the name of the Lord, and they can even give testimony of how the Lord has heard their prayers and is guiding them. They have even brought some people to the Lord.

But regardless of how pure, how spiritual, and how full of Christ his group is, it is divisive, and regardless of how poor and how weak and how short of Christ the church in San Francisco is, that is the unique church according to the ground. No one has the right to start another meeting. This is the only way for us to keep the oneness. We can never keep the oneness of the church by the spiritual condition.

Let me illustrate in another way. Suppose two Americans go to Tokyo and visit the American consulate. But from the American consulate they receive very poor service. These two are offended by such a poor consulate in Tokyo; therefore, one of them suggests that they start another American consulate in their home there. They will give the best service, they say.

Later, another American comes to Tokyo and goes to the American consulate, and he also is offended by the poor service. Then he meets the two Americans who started another consulate in their home, and they ask him to come and see how good their American consulate is. Thus, he goes to their house and finds that their American consulate just fits his taste.

You may think that this is ridiculous, but have you ever realized that this is exactly the situation of today's Christianity? Everyone is so free to start another "church" at any time and any place. But is it the proper church? It may be more spiritual, but the ground is wrong.

We know that at least thirteen million Hebrew people exist on the earth today, but only about two million have gone back to the Holy Land. In New York City alone there are at least three million Hebrews now. Are not all these just as much Hebrews as those in the Holy Land? Surely they are. But who constitutes the nation of Israel? Only those who are on the ground of the nation of Israel. Even though the number of Hebrews in New York is larger, they are still not the nation of Israel. They are Hebrews, but they are not the nation of Israel, because they are not on the proper ground. Only those who have gone back and are standing there in the Holy Land are the nation of Israel, because they are on the proper ground of their nation.

Without the Holy Land, how could the people of Israel be a nation? They simply would not have the ground. The same is true with the church. Without the proper and unique ground, how can we practice the church life? It is impossible. Therefore, in order to practice the church life, we must have the proper ground.

The Hebrews who live in New York may be fine people, very religious, and high-class people. On the other hand, those who have returned to the Holy Land may be poor and of a lower class. But if you wanted to be in the nation of Israel, would you remain in New York or return to the Holy Land? Of course, you would go to the country of Israel.

Those Hebrews who have returned to the right ground may not be so fine and so well cultured as those in New York, but I have full assurance that only with those who have gone to the Holy Land is it possible for the Lord's purpose to be fulfilled for the Hebrew nation. Regardless of how good those in New York are, they can never fulfill the Lord's purpose, for they are not on the ground of their nation.

Oh, how we need to see the importance of the ground! It is only by the ground that the oneness of the church can be kept, and it is only by the ground that we can learn the lessons we need in order to experience the reality and practicality of the church life. Without the ground it is impossible to have the proper church life.

CHAPTER NINE

THE UNIQUE GROUND OF ONENESS

Scripture Reading: Deut. 12:5-6, 8, 13-14, 17-18, 26; 14:22-23; 15:20; 16:2, 5-6, 15-16; 2 Chron. 3:1; Psa. 133

The things of the New Testament always have their types in the Old Testament. The types are pictures of that which is revealed in the New Testament, and a picture, we know, is better than a thousand words. A lengthy definition of a certain matter may still not make the matter clear, but when we look at a picture, it is immediately clear to us. This is the way the Lord teaches us. The Old Testament gives us the pictures, which are called the types; then the New Testament gives the definitions. If we are not clear regarding certain points in the definition, we can go back to the picture and compare the picture with the definition. Then everything will be exceedingly clear.

TWO WAYS OF ENJOYING CHRIST

Even the matter of the church ground has a clear picture in typology in the Old Testament. The book of Deuteronomy tells how rich the good land is, and how marvelous is the enjoyment of that land. The manna in the wilderness is a type of one aspect of Christ, and the rock in the wilderness is a type of another aspect of Christ. But the good land is the type of all the aspects of Christ. It is a complete type, an all-inclusive type, including all the rich aspects of Christ. This is the enjoyment into which the people of God must enter. But for the enjoyment of the riches of Christ as typified in Deuteronomy, God has appointed two ways. One is the enjoyment of the riches of the good land by the people individually. This is the personal and individual way. Everyone is free to enjoy the riches of the good land by themselves at any time and in any place. But there is another way, and that is the enjoyment of the riches of the good land as a corporate worship to the Lord. In this way, there is no choice as far as the place is concerned. There is only one unique place throughout the whole land of Israel chosen by God. In all the land of the twelve tribes, there is only one place that is the proper place for all the people of God to come together to enjoy the riches of the good land as a corporate worship to God. This is not the individual, but the corporate way.

In Deuteronomy the produce of the good land is divided into two parts. The first part is a tenth part, the tithe. The tithe must be the first tenth, not the last tenth. This part must be separated for the corporate worship of all the people to God. They have no right to enjoy this ten percent in any place they choose; they must bring it to the place which the Lord has chosen. This tithe is holy unto the Lord. They may prefer to enjoy it in their homes or in some other places, but they have no right to do so. They must bring this ten percent to the very place which the Lord has chosen.

The rest of the produce, the ninety percent, may be enjoyed in any place. This part is for the individual enjoyment of the riches of the good land. Thus, there are these two ways to enjoy the riches of Christ according to Deuteronomy. One is individual, and the other is corporate.

Some say that Christ is not narrow, but that He is everywhere, and this is true. I can enjoy Christ in my home, and I can enjoy Christ in any place. But this is only one way. There is another way in which we may lack. We may enjoy Christ in a private way with the ninety percent, but we cannot enjoy Christ as the firstfruit and topmost portion.

Whenever we come together on the proper ground, which is the ground ordained by the Lord, we enjoy the topmost portion of the rich Christ. We can testify this by our experience. Sometimes we pray-read in our homes and enjoy the Lord in a rich way. We feel quite satisfied. But when we come to the meetings of the local church, we see that there is no comparison. One is the topmost portion, and the other is the bottom.

Of course, everything of Christ is good, but there is still a difference between the firstfruit and the remainder.

If it were possible, I would never miss the meetings of the church in Los Angeles. I would stay in Los Angeles forever to enjoy the church meetings. I do not know how good it will be when we get into the New Jerusalem, but I believe I have enjoyed a real foretaste in the meetings in Los Angeles. There is no comparison with the topmost enjoyment of the meetings of the local church. The Holy Spirit does withhold something for the church.

There are only two ways to enjoy Christ: the individual way and the corporate way, the personal way and the Body way. Praise the Lord, there is a Body way! The people of Israel had their corn, their oil, and all the produce of the good land. They enjoyed ninety percent of all these things in their own homes and in any place they wished. Undoubtedly this was a kind of enjoyment. But I do not think they were nearly as excited with this enjoyment as they were with that of the Feast of Tabernacles. At that time, they brought the firstfruits of the produce of the good land to Mount Zion. There they met with all the people of Israel to put all the offerings together as an exhibition of the rich produce of the good land.

There were three main feasts that brought all the people of Israel to Jerusalem: the Feast of the Passover, the Feast of Weeks, and the Feast of Tabernacles. I am certain that whenever the time of these feasts arrived, all the people were moved with joy. Even before coming to Mount Zion, while they were ascending, they would sing Psalm 133:1: "Behold, how good and how pleasant it is / For brothers to dwell in unity!"

These two ways must be exceedingly clear to us. We should enjoy Christ in a personal, individual way, but we still need to enjoy Him even more in a corporate, Body way. The topmost produce of the good land is for the corporate way of enjoyment. The best portion of Christ is for our corporate enjoyment.

THE UNIQUE GROUND KEEPING THE ONENESS

With the individual way of enjoying Christ, there is no

problem, but with the corporate way, there is a real problem. Why, in the Lord's wisdom, did He make such a regulation for the worship of the people of Israel? Why was there only one place for all the people to come together to have the corporate enjoyment of the rich produce of the good land? There were twelve tribes in the good land, but the Lord only chose Jerusalem. Regardless of how far the tribe of Dan was to the north, they still had to come to Jerusalem. In Deuteronomy 12, 14, 15, and 16 the Lord said many times that the people of Israel had to worship at the place He chose. They had no choice. Moses said that in the past they all did whatever was right in their own eyes, but when they would come into the good land, they should not do what was right in their eyes, but what was right in the Lord's eyes. In other words, they could not act according to their choice, but according to the Lord's choice. Why did the Lord choose only one place for the corporate worship of the people? It was because this unique spot kept the oneness of all the people of God. This unique place was the ground of oneness.

Suppose two Israelites were neighbors living at a distance from Jerusalem in the territory of Dan. One day, they became angry with one another and eventually hated each other. However, the time of the Feast of Tabernacles was at hand, and both must go up to Jerusalem. If they did not go, they would be cut off as males from the people of Israel. Thus, they would be forced to go and must travel the same road. What could they do? Nothing remained but for them to be reconciled to each other. How else could they sing Psalm 133 as they ascended Mount Zion?

Hallelujah! The ground of oneness forces us to be reconciled to one another. The one unique ground keeps the oneness. This is why we stress again and again the local church ground. It is the one unique ground of oneness that is typified in the book of Deuteronomy.

The ground of oneness keeps all the dissenting elements away and closes all the doors to division. If we do not have the ground of oneness, I am afraid that in a few years' time there will be fifty free groups in Los Angeles. All the brothers will feel free to establish a meeting in any place they choose.

THE DEFINITENESS OF THE GROUND

It seems that it is easier for people to establish a "church" today than to open a store. If you would open a store, you must register with the government. But to establish a "church" only requires someone to start a meeting in their home. People continually refer to Matthew 18:20 as their ground for meeting. But this is wrong. To judge a church according to the presence of the Lord is never conclusive. Even the Catholic Church can testify that they have the presence of the Lord today. If you inquire of them, they will steadfastly maintain that they have the Lord's presence. But does that vindicate and justify them?

Then there are some who say that the greater the measure of Christ you have, the more you are the church. We cannot agree with this. Madame Guyon was very spiritual. Few have the measure of Christ she had. But she was not right as far as the church was concerned because she remained in the Roman Catholic Church.

Regardless of how spiritual you are, you must come to Jerusalem. Simply to love the Lord by yourself is only one aspect. There is still the corporate side. We must come to the unique ground of oneness, which is the choice of the Lord. If the standing of the church is not according to the ground but according to the so-called spiritual condition, nothing will be stable. Condition is a very relative matter. Today you may be uplifted in the spirit, but after six months you may be very low. Today I may be weak in the spirit, but by the Lord's mercy after one year, I may be strong. There is no standard of spirituality.

How spiritual is spiritual? It is similar to the length or the height. How long is the length, and how high is the height? There is no standard. But the unique ground is exceedingly definite. It is absolutely unequivocal. The standard of spirituality is extremely vague and obscure. But the matter of the ground is definite. We are one Body; so wherever we go, wherever we are, we must be in the expression of that one church. This is definite and keeps us in oneness.

Christians consider that as long as they preach the gospel

and edify the saints, they are right. But the apostles only worked with the intention of building up the local churches. There was no exception. Can anyone show from the Acts or the Epistles that one of the apostles did any work apart from that of building up the local churches? No, there is not such a hint. All the apostles went forth with the full intention of establishing, edifying, and building up the local churches.

The temple had to be built on Mount Moriah as David appointed. Mount Moriah was and still is the center of Jerusalem. It is the place where God appeared to Abraham and also to David. Abraham offered Isaac on Mount Moriah (Gen. 22:2), and David offered sacrifices to the Lord on the same spot (1 Chron. 21:18-19, 26; 22:1). Thus, David ordained that this very ground be used for the building of the temple. The people of Israel do not have the right to build the temple in any other place. They must build it on the very spot which David appointed. The church is the fulfillment of the type shown by the temple. We have no right to build a church in any place we choose. If we do, we are simply doing whatever is right in our own eyes. We will please ourselves, but we certainly will not please the Lord. Christians today continually do things which are right in their own eyes. They have no right to do so. They must build up the local church on the very ground which God has appointed, that is, the local ground.

"What you see write in a scroll and send it to the seven churches: to Ephesus and to Smyrna and to Pergamos and to Thyatira and to Sardis and to Philadelphia and to Laodicea" (Rev. 1:11). "To the seven churches" means to the seven cities. One church represents one city, and each local church is equal to that city in which it stands. To establish elders in every church is equivalent to establishing elders in every city (Acts 14:23, cf. Titus 1:5). There should be only one church in one city. In *The Normal Christian Church Life,* Brother Watchman Nee said that anything smaller than the city is not the church, and anything larger than the city is also not the church.

So many Christian workers today have altogether too much freedom. They build the "church" everywhere and on any kind of ground. There are all kinds of so-called churches:

home churches, street churches, campus churches, and so forth. All manner of churches are built upon all kinds of grounds. It is just as if every Israelite has the right to build a "temple." Benjamin builds a "temple" here, and Jonathan builds another one there. Everywhere there is a so-called temple. This is the situation of today's Christianity. There are not only many churches but many different kinds of churches. How pitiful it is!

WHO IS NARROW?

When we say that this is wrong and that we all must be one, others say that we are narrow and exclusive. But in all these years it has been proved who is narrow and exclusive. The church in the locality is not narrow. It includes all the believers in that locality. The only thing in which you may say that the church on the proper ground is narrow is that it will not take anything divisive. We will accept all kinds of Christians as long as they are saved. We will accept those who are sprinkled as well as those who are immersed. Would those who say that we are narrow receive such?

What does it mean to be narrow and exclusive? Most people simply do not know what they mean when they speak thus. To be narrow means to disregard the proper ground of oneness. If we are on the proper ground, we can never be narrow, for the ground of oneness is common to all the people of the Lord.

Some missionaries in China said to us, "We are all one in the Lord. Let us work together." But we made the situation very clear to them. We said, "Yes, we are all one in the Lord, and we are all working for Him, but there is a big difference. We are working to build up the local church, but you have been sent by your mission to come here to build up the church of your mission. This is the problem. We appreciate the fact that you have sacrificed to come to this foreign country, but you have come here to build up something other than the local church. You have come to build up the church of your denomination. It is impossible for us to agree with this. As far as gospel preaching and edifying of the saints is concerned, there is not much problem; but in building up the mission and denominational churches, we cannot go along with you. You must recognize that the building up of the mission and denominational churches is wrong. If you would relinquish this, there would be no problem."

Who is narrow? Some are narrow in their mission work. Some are narrow in their personal work. We, as the local church, are not narrow; we are broad to include all the Lord's people in our locality.

Why do the missionaries insist upon building up their mission churches in the mission fields? Why do they not give up all divisive ground and come to build the local church? When we say this, they say that we are narrow. But the Lord knows who is narrow, who is sectarian, and who is exclusive. The local church is all-inclusive. It embraces all the believers in a locality. But the problem is that so many are sectarian in their opinions and in their work. So when the local church will not take their sectarian opinions, they say that the local church is narrow.

Brothers and sisters, may the Lord be merciful to us. In such a time of confusion, we must be clear. Praise the Lord! There is no choice. Only the ground which the Lord ordains is the proper ground.

All the brothers and sisters who have been with us in these past years have tasted the real enjoyment of Christ in the church on the proper ground. Those too who have only recently begun to meet with us have sensed the sweet enjoyment there is here in the local church on the ground of oneness. It is here that the Lord has commanded His blessing, even life forever. The oil is on the Head, and the dew is on the mountains of Zion. This is the proper ground, and this is the unique place to enjoy the Lord to the uttermost.

CHAPTER TEN

ABSOLUTENESS FOR THE LOCAL CHURCH

Scripture Reading: Rom. 16:3-16; 1 Cor. 16:19; Col. 4:15-16; Philem. 1-2

THE CHURCH IN THE HOME

In order that we may be definitely clear concerning the local church (i.e., one church in one city), we must see the matter of the church in the home. Some may think that it is possible to have the church in the city and at the same time a church in the home.

In the New Testament Epistles only four homes are mentioned in which there were churches. In two of these places, it is the home of Aquila and Priscilla. The first is in Romans 16:5: "Greet the church, which is in their house." This is the house of Aquila and Priscilla. At this time they were living in Rome, and the church in Rome was meeting in their home. Therefore, the church in Rome could be called the church in their house. In fact, today in Sacramento, the church in Sacramento meets in the home of a certain brother. So we could say that there is a church in his house.

Then in Romans 16:10-11 two more houses are mentioned. But both of these verses do not mention a church. Romans 16:14 says, "the brothers with them," but it does not speak of a church. Romans 16:15 mentions "all the saints," but it also does not say that they were the church. It is just like the place that we call the Magnolia House today in Los Angeles. So many saints are living there, but we cannot say that is a church. At that time in Rome, there was only one house where there was a church, and that was the house of Aquila and Priscilla.

We must realize that the church in the home must be equal to the church in the city. There were not two churches in Rome, one called the church in Rome and another which met in the house of Aquila and Priscilla. The church in Rome simply met in the house of this couple, so there was a church in their house.

Then 1 Corinthians 16:19 says, "The churches of Asia greet you. Aquila and Prisca greet you much in the Lord, with the church, which is in their house." This again is the house of Aquila and Priscilla. Now this couple has moved from Rome to Ephesus. Acts 18:18-19 tells us this fact. So the church in Ephesus was meeting in their house. Wherever they were, this couple was so willing to have the meeting of the church in their house. In Acts 18 we see that Aquila and Priscilla traveled with the apostle Paul from Rome to Ephesus. But after Paul left Ephesus, they remained there, and the church in Ephesus met in their home. This is why the apostle Paul mentioned the church in their house.

Another church meeting in a home is mentioned in Colossians 4:15-16. Verse 15 says, "...the church, which is in his house." This is the house of Nymphas. If we read these verses carefully, we will see that the church in the house of Nymphas was the church in Laodicea. Verse 16 says, "And when this letter is read among you, cause that it be read in the church of the Laodiceans also, and that you also read the one from Laodicea."

The church in the house of Nymphas was the church in Laodicea. There was not a church in Laodicea and another church in the house of Nymphas. In Revelation 3:14 the church in Laodicea is mentioned as the only church in that city. This is the strongest proof that there were not two churches in Laodicea. There was only one church in this city, and that church was meeting in the house of Nymphas.

Now let us read Philemon 1 and 2. "Paul, a prisoner of Christ Jesus, and Timothy the brother, to Philemon our beloved and fellow worker and to Apphia the sister and to Archippus our fellow soldier and to the church, which is in your house." To understand these two verses regarding the church in the house of Philemon, we must read Colossians 4:9

and 17: "With Onesimus, the faithful and beloved brother, who is one of you" (cf. Philem. 10). "And say to Archippus, Take heed to the ministry which you have received in the Lord, that you fulfill it" (cf. Philem. 2). These two verses prove that Philemon lived in Colossae. The church in Colossae was meeting in his home. The church in his house was the church in Colossae.

The church in Rome was in the home of Aquila and Priscilla, and the church in Ephesus was also in the house of Aquila and Priscilla. Then the church in Laodicea was in the house of Nymphas, and the church in Colossae was in the house of Philemon. These are the four instances of a church meeting in a home in the New Testament.

THE VISION OF THE LOCAL CHURCH

Today Christians have too much liberty regarding the church. This is because they do not have the vision concerning the local church. If we have the vision of the local church on the right ground, we will all be restricted.

How can we practice the church life in today's confusion? How can we apply all the matters we have mentioned in the preceding chapters of this book? It all depends upon one thing: that is, *how much we have really seen the local church on the right ground.* Whenever we come to this point regarding the ground of the church, there is always a sense that we are fighting against something. I do not know why, yet in another sense I do know. Why are so many veiled when it comes to this matter? It is simply because they are so natural and religious. The natural, human, religious concept is a veil that covers us and keeps us from seeing the ground of the church.

We all need the Lord's mercy to see the local church on the right ground. Unless we see this, there is no way for us to go on. If we are only willing to be shown the local church on the right ground, the way will be opened for the Lord's mercy and grace to flood in. Regardless of how weak you are, if you are really willing to see this, the Lord will come in to bless. However, you cannot be indifferent. Do not say, "Well, the unique ground of the local church is good, but..." The Lord knows.

You may fool others, but you cannot fool the Lord. He knows
that if you say this, you are not ready for any blessing along
this line.

ABSOLUTENESS

For the local church we must be absolute and say, "Lord,
I am wrecked. I am sold. I am completely spoiled. I have no
other choice." There is no need for us to do anything if we
take this kind of attitude. In the whole universe the devil will
know where we stand, and the Lord will too.

If we are so ready, so definite, so strong, and so absolute
with the Lord's purpose in the way of the local church, the
Lord will raise up others to stand with us. But if we are
neutral and lukewarm, the Lord will do nothing. He hates
lukewarmness. Many miss the blessing of the Lord because
they are lukewarm. They say, "Yes, the denominations are
wrong, and we should not be sectarian, *but* still it is rather
difficult to have the local church. The denominations are not
the right way, but still there are problems concerning the
local church."

With spiritual things, and especially with the local church,
we must be exceedingly absolute. It is just like the case of a
married woman. If a woman marries Mr. Smith, she must
strongly declare that she is Mrs. Smith. If she says, "Well, of
course, for me to be Mrs. Jones or Mrs. Johnson is wrong, but
for me to be Mrs. Smith is still a problem," then I would ask,
"What Mrs. are you? To be Mrs. Jones or Mrs. Johnson is certainly wrong, but who are you? Are you Mrs. Smith?" If we
take this kind of attitude in our marriage, the entire blessing
of our married life will be lost.

If the denominations are wrong and the local church is
right, we must pour out every drop of our blood for it. There
is the need for absoluteness. The Lord never likes any kind
of mixture. In Genesis 1 everything is after its kind. A peach
tree must be a peach tree. An apple tree must be an apple
tree. Any kind of hybrid does not reproduce. When an apple tree
is grafted into a peach tree, it exists for one generation only.
This is the natural law.

If you feel that the denominations are right, then stay

with them and be absolute about it. But if you feel that the Lord's way is the local church, then you must be absolute. Only then will you see the blessing. The Lord is never pleased with any kind of mixture. If you feel burdened to go and work for a certain mission, you must do it absolutely. But if you are not certain that this is of the Lord, you will simply lose the ground for receiving the blessing.

We all need the Lord's mercy. We need the vision, and we need to be absolute. Once we see it, we must be willing to die for it. It is only when we are so absolute that we will have the blessing. In these last days the Lord is going to prepare His bride by recovering the local church. He is so desirous of seeing many seeking ones becoming absolute to take this way. Wherever the Lord can find even a few on this earth who are so absolute for the local church, He will pour out His blessing upon them. By His mercy we must be absolute for this way. This is the basic issue. Do not ask, "What shall I do?" Instead you must ask, "Am I absolute? Am I ready to pay the price?"

In 1937 an American brother was really seeking the Lord, and due to his seeking, he was persecuted by the other missionaries of his mission. He came to me for prayer and fellowship, and he was really helped by our meetings. Because of the war, he returned to America; but after the war, he went back to Shanghai. When he heard that I was in Shanghai at that time, he came to see me again. But he never took this way. He was so close, but he never was absolute. Sometimes the closest ones are the hardest ones. I have seen those who were far from this way; yet when they saw it, they gave their lives for it. It all depends upon the vision of the local church and our absoluteness for it.

NO COMPROMISE

Do not try to be neutral. Do not try to reconcile the denominations with the local church. You can never reconcile them. Can you reconcile black with white? You can, but it will be grey; it will neither be black nor white.

We all must be so absolute. If you feel the denominations are right, then continue in them. But if you feel they are wrong and you have seen something of the local church, then pay the full price. Never be neutral.

Some have tried their best to get us to compromise even a little. But we made it clear that that is one thing we can never do. We can never compromise. The Lord never taught us to compromise. If we like black, we take black. If we prefer white, then we take white.

All problems issue from this one thing: a lack of absoluteness. I am so glad when a sister gets married and proudly proclaims, "I am Mrs. So-and-so." This is the right principle. If we have seen the light regarding the local church, we must be absolute. We must be wrecked, spoiled, and ruined for this way. We all must learn to be absolute. We need not ask, "What should I do?" If we are absolute, ninety-nine percent of our problem has been solved. If we are absolute, we will immediately be clear, and we will know what to do.

Of course, the old ties will be cut. We will be wrecked and the bridges will be burned behind us. But I am afraid that with many the bridges are still there. They think they can experiment to see if it will work. If it will, they will stay. If it will not, they will step back over the bridge. But they will never see anything in that way, and they will never be clear. There must be no bridges behind us. Then we will be clear regarding what we must do.

When a person is so absolute and burdened with the vision concerning the local church, he will pray prevailingly. He will even pray by calling all heaven and earth to be his witness. "Lord, I call heaven and earth to witness for me. I am sold for Your purpose of the local church!" This kind of prayer will shake the darkness and will be so prevailing. Those who are absolute in this way will have the Lord's authority and the Lord's presence in a powerful way.

The way of the local church is not a small matter. Please do not be somewhat influenced and say, "Well, this is something better. I will try it." Have you realized that all the Israelites who attempted to enter the good land were not successful? Not one of them entered. Only the two who were so absolute got in. They took the attitude that regardless of how big the giants were in the land, they must enter, and they did.

Praise the Lord! If you say, "Let us try," that is the end. This is not a way for trial but a way to which we must be sold.

A LAMPSTAND

The local church is a lampstand. In the dark night it is extremely easy to find a lampstand. So many people in the Far East who have never come to the United States know where the church in Los Angeles is. The shining of the church in Los Angeles has gone throughout the whole world. In the darkness it is very easy for people to see the lighthouse. If you go to the Golden Gate Bridge in San Francisco at night, you can clearly see the lighthouse. The local church is such a lampstand. Nothing can cover it, and nothing can hide it. Do not be concerned about finding the local church in a certain city. If there is a lampstand there, it will be easy to find.

If you go to a place where there is a meeting, but there is a question regarding the ground they take, it may not be the local church. If it is the lighthouse, there is no need to question it. If you must ask, "Is this the lighthouse?" it may not be the lighthouse. We must not make our local gathering so obscure. The local church must be so definite and absolute. We should be able to say, and others should be able to say, "This is the local church." There are some places that are exceedingly ambiguous. They cause one to question whether they are the local expression of the church or not.

O brothers, may the Lord be merciful to us! No one can force us to take this way; but once we see it, no one can force us to drop it. It is so precious that we would never drop it. If we drop it, then we simply have no way to go on as a Christian. The only way to follow the Lord absolutely is to go the way of the local church.

Chapter Eleven

THE BLESSING ON THE GROUND OF ONENESS

Scripture Reading: 1 Cor. 1:10-13; 11:19; Titus 3:10; Psa. 133; Eph. 4:3

In Psalm 133 there are four main items: the oneness, the oil, the dew, and the blessing of life. Oneness causes us to enjoy the blessing of life. If we are not in oneness, of course, we miss the blessing of life. Oneness among the brothers is the very factor that brings in the blessing of life. Between oneness and life in this psalm are the oil and the dew. We know that oil in typology is the Holy Spirit, the third person of the Godhead in God's divine dispensation. But what does the dew signify? Freshness is something of the dew, but it is not the dew itself. We will see later what the dew is.

TWO ASPECTS OF ONENESS

It is quite interesting that only two aspects of the oneness are mentioned. One aspect is likened to the oil upon a body, and the other is likened to the dew which falls upon a place. In the church life, there are also these two aspects: the Body aspect and the place aspect. The church is the Body of Christ, who is the greater Aaron, and the church is also the dwelling place of God. The oil upon the Head runs down upon the Body of Christ, and the dew from Mount Hermon falls upon Zion, which is the very place of God's dwelling. So there is the Body of Christ and the dwelling place of God. With the Body of Christ is the oil, and with God's dwelling place is the dew. For both the oil on the Body and the dew on the dwelling place of God, we need the oneness. Without the oneness, there is little oil and little dew. To partake of the oil and the dew, we must have the oneness. When we are in oneness, the oil flows on the Body, and the dew falls from heaven upon the dwelling place of God. Have you ever realized that in this psalm there are these two aspects of the church life? As the Lord's Body we need the oil of the Holy Spirit flowing all the time, and as God's dwelling place we need the dew falling upon us from heaven.

Those of us who have been meeting in Los Angeles have really tasted something of this oil and dew in our practical experience. Whenever we come together, and even in our homes, we have a deep inner sense that the oil is flowing. This is the gracious moving of the Spirit. At the same time, accompanying the flow of the Spirit, is a kind of watering just as dew, so strengthening and so refreshing. In the church life there is the sweet and gracious flow of the Spirit, and at the same time, there is the watering and refreshing dew.

THE DEW OF GRACE

When we are really poor, we need mercy. But when we are in oneness, we have something more than mercy. This is the dew, the sufficient grace of the Lord Jesus Christ. "The grace of the Lord Jesus Christ and the love of God and the fellowship of the Holy Spirit be with you all" (2 Cor. 13:14). The fellowship of the Holy Spirit is the moving of the oil, and the grace of the Lord Jesus is the dew.

The more we meet together, fellowship with each other, and love one another, there is spontaneously within us a sweet flow of the Spirit, so gracious, so good, and so pleasant. At the same time we sense the strengthening within, the watering, the refreshing, the comforting and empowering. This is the grace. We have the fellowship of the Holy Spirit in the oneness, and we also have the grace of the Lord Jesus. As the Body we need the oil, and as the dwelling place we need the grace. Without the grace we are very dry. But with the grace we are watered and refreshed.

In the local church we are being watered day by day with grace, just as the fresh dew every morning. To my sense, there are no evenings in the church life. Even the evening meetings are still in the morning. Whenever we are at the Lord's table in the evening, I always sense that it is morning, because the dew is there. We do not have night, but morning with the dew. This is what accompanies the oneness of the church life.

Praise the Lord! The oil and the dew are the result of the commanded blessing of life. The Lord not only gives us the blessing, but He *commands* the blessing. It seems that the Lord on the throne orders the blessing upon those who are on the ground of oneness. I am not speaking what I do not know. I am telling you what I have experienced for the past forty years. You cannot imagine how much I have enjoyed the oil and the dew in these past years, and I am still enjoying it.

THE WAY TO KEEP THE ONENESS

What is the way for such an enjoyment? It is simply by keeping the oneness. So many today excuse themselves by saying that it was easy in the time of the apostles, but now it is not so easy. They say that it is impossible to keep the oneness, so we must not talk about it; it is enough to talk about the Lord Jesus and help others to know Him. They even say that the more we speak about oneness, the more divisions we will have. But if we are not in the oneness, we will be short of the oil and the dew. Then it will be difficult for the Lord to command the blessing of life.

How can we keep the oneness? We must see that the oneness of the Body is the oneness of the Spirit. The very Spirit Himself *is* the oneness. To keep the oneness simply means to keep the Spirit. We can only keep what we already have, so the oneness of the Spirit is already here. We only need to keep it.

But how can we keep the oneness? According to the record of the New Testament, to keep the oneness in Jerusalem was easy, for there were no other divisions, and to keep the oneness in Antioch was also easy. But to keep the oneness in Corinth was not so easy. The church in Corinth was divided into four groups: one of Paul, another of Cephas, another of Apollos, and another "of Christ." All these four groups were composed of real believers. In such a situation, how could they keep the oneness? If we were to keep the oneness with those who were of Paul, would that be the proper oneness?

They might love us, and we might love them, but it would not be the proper oneness. It would be oneness on the ground of Paul, not on the ground of oneness.

In Old Testament times, Jerusalem was the place chosen by God for His people to worship. But they were all carried away to Babylon. Suppose we were one of those in Babylon. Would we be in the proper oneness? It might be real, but it would not be proper, because the ground would be wrong; it would be the wrong place. Only the place which the Lord chooses is the proper ground of oneness.

If we went to the group of Cephas or Apollos, or even to the one that was "of Christ," the result would be the same. Regardless of how much we might love them and be one with them, the ground would be wrong. It might be real, but it would be wrong. Paul says that these are divisions.

So first of all, we must know the oneness, and we must know the proper oneness. It is impossible to keep the proper oneness in Babylon or in any divisive group in Corinth. We must come back to Jerusalem, the ground of locality. If we are in Babylon, we must come back to Jerusalem. If we are in one of the divisive groups in Corinth, we must come back to the ground of oneness in Corinth. It is impossible to have the proper oneness in any divisive group. We must come back to the one unique ground of oneness.

THE COMMANDED BLESSING

Perhaps you are by yourself. What should you do? First of all, you must get out of Babylon. Do not say that since you are alone, it is better to wait until the Lord brings others to join you. If you take this attitude, you will surely have to wait. This means that you are not absolute. If you are absolute, you will realize that it is impossible to keep the proper oneness in any kind of divisive group, regardless of how spiritual you are. You must keep yourself from anything divisive and come back to the ground of oneness. If you are really absolute and mean business with the Lord, you will experience the Lord commanding the blessing of life upon you.

When we have the oneness, there the Lord commands the blessing. Then we have the enjoyment of the oil and the dew of life. What has happened in Los Angeles is really a testimony of this. Since the brothers began to take the standing of oneness here on the ground of locality, there has been such an enjoyment of the oil and the dew! I can never forget the first conference in Los Angeles in December of 1962. The first time we sang "Oh, What a Life! Oh, What a Peace!" the roof nearly rose to the sky! There were only about seventy of us, but such a blessing of life! In all these past years, I believe the brothers and sisters have tasted the commanding of the Lord's blessing.

Do not be afraid that you will be alone. You must be faithful to Him and be absolute for the oneness. Just pray, "Lord, be merciful to me. I must take this standing of the local ground. I am not for the ground of any division but for the ground of the local church." If you take care of the standing of oneness, the Lord will take care of the commanded blessing. The Lord will raise up others to meet with you. Then you can testify to the whole universe of the blessing of oneness. The number may be small, but the oneness will be real and proper.

The brothers and sisters here can testify that by His mercy and grace we have the real brotherly love. It is not that we encourage the brothers to love. We simply have the love. This is the real oneness of Philadelphia. The Lord opens the door, and no one can shut it.

In 1932, when the Lord raised us up in north China, we were nearly all young in years. Most of us were under thirty. We began to meet on a very small scale, and the denominational leaders said, "Let them play. It will not last long." But in less than ten years, that little testimony spread throughout north China. We have heard the same thing in this country. Just recently someone said that the local church will not work here in America. But let us wait and see. It all depends upon our absoluteness and our faithfulness to the Lord.

THE KING'S BUSINESS

If this matter is our business, it means nothing. But if it is His business, it is not a small thing. The local church is indeed the King's business; so we must take a stand. Of course, some will oppose us. Nevertheless, we must take the Lord's way of oneness. If we take this way, we must be absolute. If you do not feel burdened to take this way, I do not encourage you to take it. If you feel that you have peace in going along with the denominations, just do it. But if you are going to take the way of the ground of oneness, do it in an absolute way. Do not do it lightly. We must mean business with the Lord.

We are in the Lord's recovery, and the time is short. Luke 21:24 says that Jerusalem will be trampled by the Gentiles until the times of the Gentiles are fulfilled. But Jerusalem has already been returned. I really believe that the Lord will do a quick work. We must be wise. Therefore, I believe that all the scattered brothers and sisters should come together to one or more centers. Even the students had better not study in a place without a church. The place to study is where there is a prevailing church. We must not put our studies first but put the church life first. Even our jobs do not matter. As long as we can make a living, let us be concentrated. Then we can declare to the whole world and to Satan the fact of our oneness. The oil will flow and the dew will come down, and we will see the Lord commanding His blessing. Even the gates of Hades will not be able to stand against us.

I do believe that this is the strategic way. First of all we must be concentrated, and then we must be equipped to bear the testimony and give the enemy the shame. Then we will go out to spread the oneness of the church life to other cities.

This is the way to keep the oneness. We must leave all the divisive groups and take the ground of oneness, and we must seek the Lord's leading for us to be concentrated together. Of course, no one controls this matter. We all must seek the Lord's guidance. Perhaps the Lord will lead some to meet here in Los Angeles, or with those in Akron, or with those in Houston. We all must seek the Lord's leading concerning this matter. It is only on the ground of oneness that we have the oil and the dew with the commanded blessing of life.

CHAPTER TWELVE

THE FELLOWSHIP OF THE CHURCH

Scripture Reading: 2 Tim. 2:19-21

After seeing something of the church ground, we must go on to see the fellowship of the church. Fellowship is based upon oneness, and fellowship is equal to oneness. Oneness includes and covers all the saints, regardless of the background from which they come.

ONE IN LIFE

Today there are many different backgrounds of the saints. Some have a Presbyterian background, some have a Baptist background, and some have other kinds of background. But regardless of the background, if they are saved, they all have the same faith, for they all believe in the same Lord Jesus Christ. They all have been redeemed by the same blood; therefore, they all have the same life within. We all are one in this all-comprehensive faith.

Fellowship is based upon this oneness. We have fellowship with one another because we all have the same divine life, we all have the same Lord, and we all have the same redemption. Do not ask what kind of baptism others have had. Do not talk about all those doctrines. As long as they are saints who are not sinful according to 1 Corinthians 5, we must recognize all of them as dear brothers and sisters. We believe in the Lord Jesus, and they do also. We have the same divine life as they. We have been redeemed by the blood of Christ, and they also have been redeemed by His blood. We are all the same.

We may be quite different from other Christians in background and in many other things. They may not believe in partial rapture, and we may be for it. But regardless in which kind of rapture we believe, as long as we believe in Jesus Christ as the Son of God, who was incarnated as a man, died on the cross for our sins, and resurrected from the dead, we are all redeemed, justified, regenerated and saved. We all have the divine life within us. Therefore, we are all one Body. It is based upon this that we have fellowship with one another. We may speak somewhat regarding certain things, but we must not go too far, and we must not argue. We must base our fellowship only on the Lord Himself.

THE BASIS OF FELLOWSHIP

But the problem is this: if one believes in a certain kind of rapture, he will try day and night to convince others of this doctrine. This is wrong. If some speak in tongues, we should not say anything to criticize them. Though they speak in tongues and we do not, we are still brothers. Tongues should not divide us. We may differ in the matter of tongues, but we are the *same in life*. We are all born of the same Father; so we must be one. We should not look down upon them for speaking in tongues, and they should not look down upon us for not speaking in tongues. But this is the problem. Could we receive grace from the Lord to be so general in our attitude? We must all realize that they are our brothers regardless of how much they differ from us in certain things. We must love them because we are the same as they are in redemption and in life. This is the basis and ground of our fellowship.

We may even take the unique ground of the church while others do not. But regardless even of this, we still can have fellowship with one another. However, this really requires grace. We must say, "Lord, by Your grace and mercy, I do not care for all the differences. I simply care for You. I only care for Your redemption and Your life—nothing else. Regardless of how much this brother differs from me, I still love him."

Of course, we cannot go along with any divisions. But that should not hinder our fellowship. Regardless of whether others are in the divisions or not, we must recognize that they are our brothers. This does not mean that we go along with their divisions. No, we cannot do this, but we must love all the saints, even those in the Roman Catholic Church. There are some real believers in the Roman Catholic Church, and they all have the same divine life as we. They may wear their clerical robes, but in redemption and in life we are all the same.

Why must you look down on those who speak in tongues? And why must you look down on those who do not speak in tongues? If you think speaking in tongues can help you, do it. But do not look down on those who do not do it. If you do not speak in tongues, do not look down on those who do. We really need grace to be one in this way. The fellowship of the Body and of the church is based upon one thing: that is, we all are redeemed by the same blood and regenerated by the same divine life.

Our practice is one thing, but to take our practice as a basis for fellowship is another. Our practice may be according to our need, but we should not make our practice the basis of fellowship. For instance, we love to practice pray-reading because it helps us to enjoy the Lord, but we should never make pray-reading the basis of fellowship. Whether you like pray-reading or not, we do not care. We simply love you because you are a brother.

Some who speak in tongues always like to convince others to speak in tongues. This is the problem. Some who practice baptism by immersion always like to convince others to take immersion. But we must be willing to drop all of these things as a basis for fellowship. We may practice certain things because they help us, but we should not make any practice a basis for our fellowship. We really need grace for this.

Even our way of doing things should not hinder our fellowship. The way we do things may differ from that of others. If this is the case, we should not say a word. Our way of doing things is not the basis for fellowship.

There have been some in the past who have tried to adjust us. But we have told them that since we do not adjust them, they should not adjust us. Could everyone drive a car in the same way? This is why we have "backseat" drivers. When the car is driven by you, you must drive it. But when it is driven by others, you should let them drive it. Could you do this? Could you let others drive and not say a word? It is not so easy. If you drive a car in a certain way, you should not expect others to drive it in the same way as you. Therefore, we told the dear ones who tried to adjust us that as far as we were concerned, it was quite all right for them to do things in their way. We only asked that they would please give us the same freedom to do things in our way.

We must learn the lesson of grace in this way. We may practice many things for the Lord, yet we should not make any one of these things the basis for fellowship. When we practice the church life and take the standing of the unique ground of oneness, we must not be so particular in any thing. If we become particular in any one thing, we become a sect. If you prefer to speak in tongues, you should not expect the church to speak in tongues. If you expect the whole church to speak in tongues, you will make it a sect of speaking in tongues. The church is general, very general. It cannot specialize in any particular thing. But the problem is that if the church does not take your opinion or your way, you will say that the church is narrow. But really, it is you who are narrow. We cannot take anything special. We must be general. Then we are really not narrow, but, in fact, broad.

To be broad does not mean that we take in everything. To be broad means to be general, not opposing anything nor imposing anything. If you are of a certain opinion, you should realize that not all the brothers will have the same concept. We cannot expect others always to hold the same opinion as we.

We must be general. We should not be particular in anything. Wherever you go, do not make demands upon others. Perhaps their way is better than yours, or yours better than theirs, but this is not important. We must be general so that we may have the proper fellowship. The proper fellowship is not based upon a way or a practice. It is only based upon the same life within us.

Why must we always attempt to convince others? Why must we make them the same as we? As long as we all believe in the same Lord and are on the ground of oneness, any kind of practice which is not sinful is tolerable. We must learn to give others the freedom to do things in their way.

We should never make anything a basis of fellowship. We must respect every local church, realizing that it has its own jurisdiction. San Francisco may prefer to use wine at the Lord's table, but another place may prefer grape juice. We must give them the freedom to use whatever they choose.

Why do we need to draw attention to this matter? It is because we have seen in the past that these things have created much trouble. That is why we must be general. Only the Lord Himself can be our basis for fellowship.

IDENTIFIED WITH ALL THE CHILDREN OF GOD

There is another problem which we must notice. Some brothers who have seen the ground of the local church feel that if they take this ground, they will be cut off from the fellowship of other groups of Christians. Not too long ago, a brother asked me this question: "How can we take the ground of the local church yet still be identified with all the people of the Lord?" I answered that it is impossible. Why is this so? It is simply because today is a day of division.

For example, we know that before the captivity, all the people of Israel lived in the land of Canaan. At that time, it was possible for everyone to be identified with all the people of God. But at the time of captivity, some were carried away to Egypt, some to Syria, and the majority to Babylon. Thus, they were divided. In this kind of situation, how could *one* Israelite be identified with *all* the people of Israel? If he were identified with all those in Babylon, he would be cut off from those in Egypt and Syria. If he were identified with the group in Egypt, he would be cut off from those in Babylon and Syria.

Today it is impossible to identify ourselves with all believers. Do you think you could be identified with the saints in the Roman Catholic Church? It is impossible. However, it is not a matter of being identified with all saints. It is a matter of taking the command of the Lord to return to the proper ground. At the expiration of the seventy years, the Lord commanded all the Israelites to return to Jerusalem. We also must take the Lord's command to return to our "Jerusalem." We can never be identified with all the Lord's people today, because so many will not obey the Lord to come back to the ground of oneness.

Even if we did not take the ground of the church, we could never be identified with all the children of God in the present situation of division. It is impossible, because all the children of God are divided, separated, and scattered. What we must do today is not to be identified with all the Lord's people but to take the way of the Lord's recovery by coming back to the original ground. We would like to fellowship with all the saints, but the situation today does not allow us to do so.

There is really no need of taking this matter into consideration. As long as we are willing to be general and ready to fellowship with all the saints, that is sufficient. Whether or not we can identify with all the saints is not *our* responsibility but *their* responsibility. They all must come back to "Jerusalem."

PROPER ONENESS ON THE PROPER GROUND

If all the saints would return to "Jerusalem," there would be no problem. The problem is that some are willing to come back, but the majority are not willing to come back. Should we remain then in the divisions? No, we must come back to the ground of oneness. Others will say that by so doing we create more divisions. They will say that before we came back to the proper ground, there were not as many divisions, but after we returned, there is a further division. They will say that we have increased the number of divisions. But we should not take this kind of accusation. Actually, we are not causing a division but rather recovering the proper oneness. The proper oneness can only be on the proper ground. To remain in the denominations is to keep the divisions. When we return to "Jerusalem," we return to the proper oneness and are not responsible for any division. Who then is responsible? It is those who will not come back to the original ground of oneness.

In 1937 in Chefoo, north China, I was invited to a dinner with some Christian leaders. Nearly all the leaders of the denominations of that city were there. After a time they said, "Brother Lee, we have heard you say that we all must be one.

But the more you speak about oneness, the more you create division." Then I answered, "Brothers, we all know that the believers in Corinth were divided. Some said they were of Paul, some of Apollos, some of Cephas, and some even of Christ. But all were rebuked by the apostle Paul. In the light of this I would ask you if you think it is right for me to call myself a Presbyterian or a Lutheran or a Baptist?" They replied, "No, we would not ask you to do that." So I said, "What then shall I do? Since you do not ask me to be a Presbyterian, a Lutheran, or a Baptist, what shall I do, and where shall I go?" They could not answer me. I continued: "Since I love the Lord, I must preach the gospel, and undoubtedly there will be some who will be saved through my preaching. Since you have said that I should not be in any denomination, should I send those who have been saved through me to a denomination which I cannot join?" Still they could not answer me. Then I boldly said, "So you see, we are forced to take the ground of oneness so that we can meet together in the proper way. You say that we cause division, but who is responsible for the divisions? If all of you will promise me to drop all the denominational names and divisive elements and come together as the local church in this city, I will immediately ask the brothers to close our meeting hall. At this they shook their heads and said that this would be impossible. So I said very strongly, "Who then is responsible for the divisions?"

We must not take this kind of accusation. People insist on their divisions, yet they condemn others for creating more divisions. A number of the Israelites did go back to Jerusalem. Apparently, they increased the number of groups. But *actually,* they did not bear the responsibility for divisions. It was those who insisted upon remaining in captivity and not obeying the command of the Lord to go back to Jerusalem who were responsible for the divisions among the Lord's people.

CHAPTER THIRTEEN

PRACTICAL LESSONS FOR THE CHURCH LIFE

Scripture Reading: 1 Tim. 3:15

WHAT TO DO WITH DENOMINATIONS

In the last chapter we have seen something regarding the attitude we must have toward the saints who are still in the denominations. On one hand, we must be so general and so open to all saints regardless of their background. But on the other hand, if they are still in the denominations, it is rather difficult for us to identify ourselves with them. However, the responsibility is not ours but theirs. As long as we return to the proper ground of oneness, we are absolved from all responsibility of division. For this reason we can do nothing to help them. All we can do is to return to the proper ground. Positionally speaking, this is the right place for us to be identified with all the children of God. But actually speaking, it is impossible because so many of them are still in the divisions.

Now we must see what we should do with the denominations. Some brothers who have seen that the denominations are wrong still insist that we must stay there. They say that if we do not remain in the denominations, we will be charged with causing division. They also say that we must stay to help others, for if we leave, there will be no way to help them. At least some who have seen that the denominations are wrong speak in this way. I know some dear saints who are like this.

Well, are the denominations right or wrong? If they are wrong, should we stay in them? Should we remain in something wrong? If you cannot leave because others will say that you cause division, I am afraid you are the biggest politician

on earth. You are not faithful to what you see. You know the
denominations are wrong, yet you still remain because you
are afraid of what others will say. This is not honest or faithful.

You may say that we must be careful not to cause divisions. But to leave Babylon and return to Jerusalem is not
causing a division. To abandon what is wrong and come back
to what is right is not causing a division. We all must have a
pure conscience. Regardless of how much you say you are
careful, I say that you are political. In your heart you condemn the denominations, yet you still remain there. I do not
believe that Christians should hold this kind of attitude. If
you stay, what kind of work will you do? Will you stay in
a denomination and do a work which is absolutely against
that denomination? We should not be this kind of person.

The Presbyterians, for example, exert much energy to
build up their Presbyterian denomination. If you agree with
them, you should stay. But if you do not agree with them, you
should plainly tell them that you cannot stay. We must be
honest. We should not pretend that we are one with a certain
denomination, yet day by day undermine it. This is not right,
and this is not honest. Eventually, all such people will be
expelled by the denominations. Suppose you are a pastor of a
denomination. Would you allow a member of your denomination to remain and yet undermine your work? You would have
to dismiss him.

Everything must be after its kind according to Genesis 1.
If we are for the denominations, we must remain with the
denominations. But if we are not for them, we must be faithful and honest to tell them so.

In 1927 I was elected a member of the executive commit-
tee of the denomination I was in. But I told them frankly that
I could not accept the position and that I was going to leave
them. That was the end of my denominational life. I still
believe that this way is right. We are the children of light,
and we must be honest to ourselves and to others.

We must abandon the idea of remaining in the denominations to help others. If we stay, we are not honest. Suppose
you are a missionary, and the mission sends you out as a

missionary to work for that mission. You must be honest to them. If you work honestly and faithfully for the mission, you are right. You should not go to the field yet work in another way. This is not honest. You may say that you are doing something for Christ, but I do not believe the Lord needs such underhanded servants.

We must be after our kind. If we are denominational, we must be one hundred percent denominational. If the denominations are wrong, we must leave them at any cost. We have to be what we are. We should not pretend to be something. That is being political. Let us be so simple, so faithful, and so honest to God, to others, and to ourselves. We must let people know what we are and where we stand. We should not pretend to be anything. If we prefer the denominational way, then we must stand for it. The Lord never respects pretension. We must be what we are.

Of course, if we are so frank, we may offend some people. But eventually, if we do not declare what we are, we will offend them more. From the beginning we must let others know what we are and where we stand. I say this because it is so easy to consider it better to remain in the denominations. I frankly tell you that this does not work.

There are some who say this is right. They agree that they should not stay in the denominations to undermine their work. But they say that we must stay to pray for them and improve them. This is a good intention, but I have never seen anyone who has succeeded in so doing. If you do not believe my word, you may go and waste your time. Try a few years and see whether you can improve them. I am sure that you cannot. We must not involve ourselves in so many things; it is just a waste of time.

NOT FOR DOCTRINES, FORMS, OR PRACTICES

Now we must see some of the practical lessons of the church life so that we may know how to behave in the local church.

When we leave the denominations and come to the ground of oneness, we must learn immediately that we are not for any doctrine, form, or practice. We are absolutely for Christ as life. We can never stress this point too much. We are not here for anything but Christ as our life. We are not here for any doctrine, form, or practice. Why must I emphasize this one thing? It is because this helps to deliver us from our different opinions in these three categories. It is so easy to have different opinions regarding doctrines, forms, and practices.

Suppose you are in Sacramento and you leave the denomination that you are in. You discover that a group of believers are meeting on the proper ground in Sacramento, and you proceed to meet with them. Suppose, then, that you find there something that you do not agree with. They may pray-read very loudly, and you may feel that you simply cannot go along with that. What then would you do?

We must remember that on the proper ground we do not stand for any doctrine, form, or practice. We only stand for Christ as life. We must not care whether they have pray-reading or something else. As long as it is not sinful, it is all right. If they minister Christ as life, we will receive the proper help. We must not oppose or impose anything, but simply minister Christ as life to them in a living way.

When you go to a church and simply minister Christ as life, you will be no problem. If they do something that you do not like, you must not say a word. Whatever they do, you should not care. All you must seek to do is to minister Christ as life to them. The longer you stay there, the more the church will be nourished, strengthened, and built. All the saints there will be so happy that the Lord has sent you to them. If you go there to criticize their pray-reading and everything they do, you will only damage yourself and the church. This will really frustrate the fellowship in that church. We all must realize that on the church ground, we are here for nothing but Christ as life. We are not for any doctrine, form, or practice.

NEVER ADJUSTING

Another lesson we must learn is never to adjust others. As long as their behavior is not sinful, we should leave them alone. To be sinful is one thing, and to be wrong is another. For instance, the best time for us to meet during the weekdays may be 7:30 P.M. But suppose the leading brothers decide to have the meeting at 7:00 P.M. This may be wrong, but it is not sinful. Suppose that such a decision is made. Would you say anything? Could you come joyfully without saying a word? You may say that this is asking too much, but we need something which is too much to test us. Then we will know where we are.

It is far too easy for us to criticize and say something. It is really difficult to be quiet in the church life. The car you drive can be driven in your way. But if you are not behind the steering wheel, you must allow others to drive. You may think that if only you were in the position of responsibility, everything would be right. But the Lord has sovereignly placed others in this position. This is a test to see if you are really for the church life.

You may say that the leading brothers in your church are not so good. But I can tell you that *every* leading brother is not so good. There is not one exception. If you cannot go along with those where you are, you will never be able to go along with those in other places.

Wherever we are in a local church, regardless of how wrong they are, we must go along with them as long as they are not sinful. Of course, if the leading brothers put up an idol and say that we all must worship it, we must stand against this because it is sinful. To hold something which is sinful is one thing, but to do something which is wrong is another. It is rather difficult to ascertain the standard of right and wrong. What is the standard for right, and what is the standard for wrong? It is really difficult to know.

ABANDONING THE AMBITION FOR POSITION

Another thing we must learn to abandon is the ambition for position. In the church life there is the temptation of wanting to take the lead. We all are human. You may say that you do not want to be a leading brother. In a sense I believe you, but in another sense I do not believe you. If the church puts you in a position, though you say that you do not like it, you are still so happy about it, and if the church does not put you into a position, you *say* that you do not care, but you really do. You simply feel unhappy. The Lord knows, and you know too. You feel that you are older, more experienced, and more qualified than others. Why are they in the position and you are not? Perhaps you do not say this to others, but it is deep in your heart.

I have been this kind of "doctor" for many years. I know all the cases. When you come to me and say you are healthy, I know that you have tuberculosis. What kind of tuberculosis? It is simply the tuberculosis of being jealous of those who are in leading positions. You would not say it, but you feel it. There is something secret, something hidden, within you. If the church were to put you into a leading position, you would function so much in the meetings. But since the church has not given you such a place, you come with your mouth shut. This is all because of the self-seeking ambition within you.

When we come to a local church, we should never consider that we must be an elder or a deacon. Whether we are an elder or a deacon does not really mean anything as long as we minister Christ as life to others. Even if we have no position at all, we should not care. We should just minister Christ continually to others without saying a word about the brothers who are taking the lead.

I realize that we all love the Lord and the church. But deep within all of us, there is the germ of ambition, which must be dealt with. If we do not deal with this kind of ambition, the fellowship and the church life will be damaged.

To talk about the church life is easy, but when we practice it, we will see that everything will test us. No place in the entire earth exposes a person like the local church. The church exposes everything. We could never be exposed so thoroughly in any other place. The church even exposes the intent within our heart. Nothing can be hidden.

Sometimes people argue about doctrine, but this is just an excuse. If they were given a certain position in the church, even the wrong doctrine would not bother them! How can we have proper fellowship if we are like this? It is impossible. Whether we have a position or not, we should be happy that we are in the church life. Then it will be very easy to go along with the brothers and sisters.

These are the lessons we must learn. We must not insist on anything, we must not expect to be anything, and we should never try to adjust anyone. The secret is just to be so simple. Whatever the church does, whatever the brothers and sisters do, we should not care. We must simply love them and minister Christ to them, as well as receive the help of Christ from them. We should just go along with the church, whatever it does. Then the fellowship of the church will be a strong testimony to others.

I pray that all of these small matters will become very clear to us. May we be wise regarding "the little foxes" that secretly damage the church life. We all must realize these things and be saved from them. We must not care for any doctrine, form, or practice; we must not try to adjust others; and we must not desire any position in the church. We must simply love the Lord and the church and learn to minister Christ as life to others and receive help in life from others. This is the proper way we should take in the practice of the church life.

CHAPTER FOURTEEN

THE FUNCTION OF THE CHURCH

To each one of us grace was given according to the measure of the gift of Christ. Therefore the Scripture says, "Having ascended to the height, He led captive those taken captive and gave gifts to men." (Now this, "He ascended," what is it except that He also descended into the lower parts of the earth? He who descended, He is also the One who ascended far above all the heavens that He might fill all things.) And He Himself gave some as apostles and some as prophets and some as evangelists and some as shepherds and teachers, for the perfecting of the saints unto the work of the ministry, unto the building up of the Body of Christ, until we all arrive at the oneness of the faith and of the full knowledge of the Son of God, at a full-grown man, at the measure of the stature of the fullness of Christ, that we may be no longer little children tossed by waves and carried about by every wind of teaching in the sleight of men, in craftiness with a view to a system of error, but holding to truth in love, we may grow up into Him in all things, who is the Head, Christ, out from whom all the Body, being joined together and being knit together through every joint of the rich supply and through the operation in the measure of each one part, causes the growth of the Body unto the building up of itself in love. (Eph. 4:7-16)

To have a proper expression of the church, we need the proper function. What has caused the shortage of the church life is that the church has no function. We must realize that all the divisions with their forms, knowledge, and doctrines work together to damage the function of the church. When a physical body is divided, how can it function? When the Body is split, all the functions are gone. The subtlety of Satan is simply to kill the function of the Body. As long as we are divided, we are through as far as function is concerned.

NO FUNCTION IN CHRISTIANITY

The forms in today's Christianity kill the function of the church. Nearly all the members of different denominations have become pew members. There is no function; so they are called laymen, which means that they do not function. They consider that they are not the experts. This is the subtlety of the enemy.

When knowledge, teachings, and doctrines replace life, there is no function. We may have much knowledge but be short of life. When the Body is short of life, it is difficult to function. Function requires the growth in life. If a person does not grow, it is impossible for his body to function. Therefore, knowledge, doctrines, and teachings kill the functions of the Body. The Bible says, "The letter kills, but the Spirit gives life" (2 Cor. 3:6). If you are killed, how can you function? This is why we say again and again that we must turn from doctrine to the Spirit. The letter kills, but the Spirit gives life. As long as we have life, we will grow, and the more we grow, the more we will function.

Oh, the subtlety of the enemy! He uses divisions, forms, doctrines, teachings, and knowledge to kill the functions of the Body and to paralyze it. This makes the Body useless and meaningless. This is the real situation of today's Christianity. All Christianity is paralyzed because there is no function.

THE RECOVERY OF THE BODY'S FUNCTION

But, praise the Lord, in His recovery He is recovering all the functions of the Body in the local churches. Without the functions in the local church, the local church is without meaning. If believers come together without functioning, what is that? It is certainly not the church. In the practical church life there is a desperate need of functioning. We need the functions of all the brothers and sisters. All who partake of the church life must be functioning members. When everyone functions, we will have a strong, living, practical, and aggressive church life.

The proper building up of the church life depends upon our functioning. Suppose five hundred brothers and sisters are meeting in Los Angeles on the church ground, and ninety-nine percent of them fail to function. They are simply pew members, and only five brothers who are professional do all the functioning. I do not know what to say about this kind of situation. Perhaps they are on the church ground, but they are paralyzed on the church ground. They must be a social group, a religious society, or a kind of organization, for the people are put together without functioning. Just a group of people is an organization. It is not an organism until all the members are functioning and growing together. Then it will be an organism instead of an organization and a Body instead of a group. I hate to hear people call us a group. It is a shame if we are just a group. We must realize that we are a Body. What is a body? A body is an organism with all its members functioning in a living way. While I am speaking, not only is my mouth exercised, but my whole body is functioning. This is the body, not a group of bones put together. It is a shame to be called a group. We must be a living Body.

Suppose fifty percent of the members of my body function, and the other fifty percent are not functioning. What kind of body is this? It is paralyzed. With but one shoulder out of function, the body feels very awkward. Even if only a little finger does not function, the body feels the inconvenience. If you do not believe me, cut off your little finger, and you will see how awkward it is. All the members need to function, and then we will have a living, strong, and aggressive local church. All the members of the Body must function. We do not have a pastor, but we have everyone functioning. We have brothers functioning, and we have sisters functioning. We all need to function, for without functioning, we cannot have a proper church life.

THE WAY TO FUNCTION

How can we function? As we have mentioned previously, oneness is first, life is second, and fellowship is third. This is why we must repudiate, renounce, and reject all divisions. The Lord will honor this. We must come back to the oneness, and we must grow in life. Then we must have the proper fellowship. Today there are mainly two kinds of believers: one kind is in the denominations including the Roman Catholic Church, and the other is composed of those who are out of the divisions and on the proper ground. We must know how to deal with these two kinds of believers—this is the fellowship. We must know how to fellowship with the saints in the different denominations including the Roman Catholic Church, and we must know even more how to fellowship with the believers who are standing on the proper ground to fight the battle for the Lord's kingdom.

It is based upon the oneness, the life, and the fellowship that we function, and the real function is the real building up. The local church is built up by the function of all the members. In Ephesians 4:7-16 we see that the Head does not build up the local church, which is the expression of the Body of Christ, directly. He builds the local church through the gifted persons such as the apostles, prophets, evangelists, and shepherds and teachers. Moreover, even the gifted persons do not build up the Body directly. They build up the church indirectly through all the members. Eventually, it is only the members who build up the church directly.

Therefore, if the brothers and sisters do not function, the members are not building. Then how can the church be built up? It is impossible. The Head would not do it, and the gifted persons should not do it. If they do, they become the clergy. The building must come from the functioning of all the members of the Body.

A TRAIN OF VANQUISHED FOES

In these few verses in Ephesians 4, many matters are covered. First of all, verse 8 speaks of the victory gained by the Head. Without this victory Christ the Head has no position to give gifts to the Body so that we can have the different functions. Ephesians 4:8 says that Christ has led captive those taken captive. Do you know what this means? It is rather difficult to understand. This is not an adequate translation; it gives the impression, mistakenly, that Christ has brought back those who have been captured by Satan. This is not the right meaning. The Amplified New Testament gives the best rendering: "Therefore it is said, When He ascended on high, He led captivity captive [He led a train of vanquished foes] and He bestowed gifts on men." This means that Christ has captured all of His enemies. He won the victory on the cross and defeated Satan and all His enemies. Then after resurrection, while He was ascending into the heavens, He led a train of vanquished foes who had been defeated by Him. This is the right meaning of this verse. Then He had the position to give gifts to the Body.

However, we must apply this principle to ourselves. Has Christ defeated you? I am afraid that Christ has not defeated you, so you cannot be led in His train of defeated foes. You will not let Christ have the victory. Christ is victorious in the whole universe but not in you, because you have not been subdued by Him. This is why you do not function.

Some may ask, "How can I function in the Body?" From Ephesians we see that you must first be subdued by Christ. You must be conquered by Christ. If you have not been conquered and subdued by Christ, you cannot have any function. You must pray from the depth of your being, "Lord, I surrender. I am defeated by You. I am captured by You." If you really mean this, the Lord will become so living to you, and you will become so living in the meetings.

Sometimes, some of the brothers do not pray in the meetings. If we ask them why they do not pray, they may give us this excuse or that. But the real reason is because they have not been captured by Christ. If they will surrender to Christ and let Him lead them in His train of defeated foes, they will be the first to pray in the meetings.

THE GROUND FOR THE GIFT

We all need to be defeated, captured, and gained by Christ. If we have been captured by Christ, He has the ground to give us the gifts; but if we still have not surrendered to Him to be captured by Him, He has no ground to give us the gifts. We must be willing to surrender and be captured by Him. We must be the first foe in His train of defeated ones. Then He will have the ground to give us the gifts.

The gift is the basis for the function. The function comes out of the gift. Ephesians 4:11 says, "He Himself gave some as apostles and some as prophets and some as evangelists and some as shepherds and teachers." Perhaps the Lord's intention is to establish you as a teacher in the church, but to this very day He cannot do it because you will not give Him the position. You still are not captured by Him. You still are not subdued by Him. You still have not surrendered to Him. Though He intends to establish you as a teacher in the church, you will not give Him the ground to do it. When you are willing to be subdued and captured by Him, you will give Him the ground to give you the gift and establish you as a teacher.

GROWTH IN LIFE

For the gift we need the grace, and the grace is given according to the gift. With the gift is the capacity to receive the grace. The grace is the life; so to have the capacity as a teacher, we need to grow. Our two eyes and our two arms are gifts to our body, but the capacity of the eyes to receive blood is much smaller than that of the arms. This means that blood is given according to the capacity of the members. This is the meaning of Ephesians 4:7: "To each one of us grace was given according to the measure of the gift of Christ." The grace is given according to the measure of the gift. If you are a bigger gift, you have a larger capacity to receive the grace. If you are a smaller gift, you have a smaller capacity to receive the grace. Grace is the life supply. A boy has two eyes, but he needs to grow. To grow means to receive more supply. When his two eyes are full of the life supply, they will be full of the growth in life. It is this growth in life that will afford the function to his eyes. First, we must be captured by Christ; then the gift will be given to us. Then we need to grow in life. The more we grow in life, the more we will receive the life supply, and the more this life supply will afford us the function.

Suppose a brother has been captured by Christ and has

given Christ the authority to establish him as a teacher, but after this he does not grow. Then he is a teacher who cannot function so well. It is just the same as the boy's eyes: his eyes will not function so well if he is short of the life supply. Here a brother has been established by the Head, but he cannot function adequately because he is short of life. But suppose this brother, by holding the reality, begins to grow into the Head in all things (v. 15). Then he will not only be a teacher, but a teacher full of life. This rich, abundant life will afford him a rich function.

EVERY MEMBER A GIFT TO THE BODY

If we compare Ephesians 4 to Psalm 68, we see that there was a battle fought by Christ in the universe, and Christ has defeated all His enemies. He led all the defeated foes in His victory train while He was ascending to the heavens. Therefore, He has gained the ground to fill all things in the universe. Christ has gained the ground in the universe, but has He gained the ground in you? You must be captured by Him. You must be defeated and fully taken over by Him. Then He will have the ground in you to make you a gift.

The gift in Ephesians 4 differs from the gift in Romans 12. In Romans 12 the gift is the ability, but in Ephesians 4 the gift is the person as a member of the Body. All the members are gifts to the Body. My little finger is a real gift to my body. Without it I am short of something. Without my two eyes I lack the ability to see. The two eyes are gifts to my body. The Lord has given my body two eyes that I may see, and He has given two legs that I may stand. In like manner, all the members of the Body of Christ, the church, are gifts to the church. Every member is a gift, but this gift must be established by the Head by being captured by Him. The Lord's intention is to give you as a gift to the Body, but if you would not be captured by Him, He can never establish you as a gift. Not until you are willing to be captured by Him will He have the ground and standing to make you such a gift.

There is a real shortage in the elders of nearly every local church. There are not many efficient elders. Why is this? It is because so many dear brothers would not be captured by the

Head. They may pay the price to give up the denominations and come back to Jerusalem to take the ground of oneness in the local church. But when they come to this point, they must be captured by the Head. They must be absolutely defeated and taken over by the Head. But so many are not willing. They say, "Lord, wait a little while; I am not ready yet." They may not say this outwardly, but this is their feeling within.

We may pay the price to take the way of the church life, but when we come to the matter of being subdued by the Lord, a real quarrel exists between us and the Lord. This is the reason that so many dear ones are not able to function in the local churches. You may say that a certain brother is a good brother. Yes, he is a good brother. You may say that he loves the Lord. Yes, to a certain extent he loves the Lord. But why is he not able to function? It is simply because the Lord has not yet gained the victory in him. He must give the ground to the Lord, and then he must grow. It is only by being captured by the Lord that the Lord will establish this brother as an elder. Then by the growth in life, the function of an elder will be manifested. The living function will be manifested because he has been captured by the Head and is growing in Him.

NOT THE CAPABILITY BUT THE LIFE

Do not think that the elders in the church must be persons with certain natural qualifications and capabilities. No, that is not what the church needs; that is what worldly organizations need. Worldly organizations need someone with a capable and clever mind and a good character. Some may say that this kind of person would make a good elder. But he is not a good elder; he can only be a good chairman in a certain society. He is a good manager, but he is not a good elder for the church.

In 1944 the war in China was nearly ended. There was a man who was highly educated and qualified in government work and whom some of the brothers were trying to bring to the Lord. It was quite probable that he would be saved. Then the brothers told Brother Watchman Nee that if such a man with his qualifications were saved, surely he would be the best for the church. But Brother Nee said, "No, he is only good for government work. He is not good for the church." What the church needs is not capable or qualified men. They can build up the tower of Babel, but they cannot build up the church of Christ.

What the church needs are those who have been captured, subdued, conquered, fully possessed by Christ, and then are growing in Him in all things. Do not think that you can do things satisfactorily if you hold responsibility in the church. You may do everything right, but you are not the proper person to hold responsibility, because you have never been captured by Christ nor grown into Him. To do things right is one thing, but to have the flow of life is another.

One day in 1948 the church in Shanghai had a large love feast. There was a sister serving who was exceedingly capable; she did everything right. But you could only sense her capability; you could not sense much life in her. She was so capable in doing things. She would really be good for the Y.W.C.A., but she was not so good for the church.

It is not the capability that matters but the life expressed. In the church it is not doing things rightly that is required but the rich flowing out of life. This is all the church needs. The church needs a group of elders who are full of life. Some of the brothers must be willing to be fully captured by Christ and to grow in Him all the time. The flow of life from these brothers is the function.

This is why I stress again and again that we must not care for what is right and what is wrong. We must not care for the teachings or regulations. Regardless of how much you know or regulate, there still may be no life. We are an organism, not an organization. We are a building with living functions, not a brick building without life. What the church requires is the flow of life, for the function of all the members is in this flow. When you come to the meeting of the church and pray something regarding the Lord, all the brothers and sisters must sense the flow of life. When you go to visit a family, perhaps you will not say much, but if life flows out, you will water and refresh them. This is the function, and this function requires the ground given to the Head and the growth in life. We all must be captured and possessed by Christ and grow in life so that we may function.

NEVER REPLACING THE MEMBERS

Regardless of how great a gift you are, you cannot replace the members. You are just a part of the Body; you cannot replace the Body. If you have the gift of an apostle or prophet, you should not substitute or replace all the other members. What you should do is perfect them. All the apostles, prophets, evangelists, and shepherds and teachers are given for the perfecting of the saints. Then the saints must function to build the church. In Ephesians 4:12 there is one *for* and two *unto*s: "*For* the perfecting of the saints *unto* the work of the ministry, *unto* the building up of the Body of Christ." If you have the gift of an apostle or prophet, you should not replace the saints but do a perfecting work to perfect the saints. The perfecting of the saints is *unto* the work of the ministry.

Let me illustrate in this way. Suppose you are a gift as a prophet or apostle to the church. Before you came, all the brothers simply did not know how to pray in the meetings. Yet, after you came, you are the only one who prays in the meetings. All the brothers and sisters appreciate your prayers so much. We must be clear that this substitution and replacement is wrong. Perhaps before you came, many of them would not pray in the meetings. But if you would perfect them properly, after a certain time everyone would be praying in the meetings. You come not to replace but to perfect them to function.

It is not easy to change our concept. I believe that today some brothers and sisters are settled already. They think, "Let Brother Brown do this, or let Brother Smith do that, or let Brother Jones handle that." This is wrong. All the gifted persons must perfect the saints unto the work of the ministry, unto the building up of the Body. Those who take the lead must be extremely careful not to do anything to replace or substitute others.

"OUT FROM WHOM"

Ephesians 4:16 says, "Out from whom all the Body." The supply comes out from Christ, into whom we have grown as our Head. We have grown into Him, and now something flows out from Him. The *into* in verse 15 goes along with the *out from* in verse 16. First, we must grow *into* Him; then *out from* Him will come something to build the Body. Out from Him the whole Body fitly joins together, the joints supply, and every part has a measure. This means that every member has a measure. That is why we must grow and grow and grow, and this is why we stress life again and again. We all must grow into the Head; then out from the Head we will receive something to minister to the Body for the building up of the local church.

We must forsake the concept that we are coming to the meeting simply to get help from the gifted persons. This is something from our background. If we are going to have a proper church life, we must give up the clergy-laity system, give up ourselves to let Christ take over, and give up the concept that we come to the meetings to receive help from those who are gifted. I should come to the meeting as a member of the Body who has grown into the Head so that out from Him I have something to minister to the Body. Then, while I am ministering to the Body, I will also receive the ministry from the other members. This is the function that builds up the church.

NO EXPERTS IN THE CHURCH

When I was in Pittsburgh in 1964, a brother said, "O Brother Lee, in this modern day we need experts in every business; so for the church service we also need experts. We need some brothers to be full time experts; the rest simply do not have the time to take care of the church service. We are busy with our education and occupations, and the sisters are busy with their families and homes. We do need some experts for the church service." But I told this brother that this is the clergy of the denominations, not the priesthood of the local church.

Some may say, "It is too hard to be a member in the local church. You must give yourself to be captured by Christ and grow. You also must give up the concept of getting help from others but go to the meetings to minister something yourself.

This is too much. I cannot go this way. I like to be an easy Christian. I work five days a week, and when Sunday comes I need to rest a while. I want to go to a church where I can sit to enjoy others' ministry. That is the time for the experts to do their job and for me to enjoy their work. I do not like your kind of church. I must give up this and give up that; I have to do this, and I have to do that. It is simply too much."

I sympathize with those who say this, but there is no other way. To them it is a hard job, but to us it is a real enjoyment. It is an enjoyment to give up ourselves; it is an enjoyment to be captured and gained by Christ; and it is an enjoyment to come to the meetings to minister something of Christ as life to others. Some may say that this is difficult, but we say that it is our best enjoyment. It all depends upon the concept we have, and it also depends upon the taste we have. If we have a taste for the organizational way of sitting and listening, we cannot have the proper church life. Our taste must be for the living function of all the members of the Body in the local church. When all of the members function, we will become a living organism, fighting the battle for the Lord's recovery. Otherwise, we simply have a group of brothers and sisters as a kind of organization.

May the Lord be merciful to us so that we all may be so willing and aggressive to have the proper functions in the church.

CHAPTER FIFTEEN

FUNCTIONING
BY PUTTING OFF THE OLD

Scripture Reading: Eph. 4:13-16, 22-24; Col. 2:6-7; 3:10-11

We have pointed out that if we are going to have the proper function in the local church, we need first of all to be captured by Christ. Christ must exercise His victory over us. If we are not defeated by Him, it is impossible to have a real spiritual function in life. This is because the function of the Body is simply the expression of Christ. In order to have the expression of Christ, we must be subdued, captured, and taken over by Christ, and after being captured by Him, we must grow in Him. The more we grow in Him, the more we will receive of Him our function in the church.

The function must come completely out of Christ. If we are devoid and short of Christ, we may have many activities, but we do not have any function in life. Some dear ones in the church only have activity, but this is not the function of life. Activity is natural. Perhaps I am clever and capable in speaking; so I stand up to give a message. But this is not the function in life; this is an activity of the natural man. All such activities are not good for the church; they are only good for some social organization. They are not good for the expression of Christ, because the expression of Christ is simply Christ manifested through His members.

Therefore, we, His members, must be captured and taken over by Him. We must grow, not only in Him but also with Him. The real essence of growth in life is nothing less than Christ Himself. Then we will have the function with Christ in life.

PUTTING OFF AND PUTTING ON

The above verses in Ephesians and Colossians set forth a number of principles concerning our function in the church. One of the basic principles is the putting off of the old man and the putting on of the new.

I am afraid that many of us have been Christians for years, but have never learned the practice of putting off and putting on. Some may ask, "Put off what?" We must put off the old man. Some may ask, "What is the old man?" The apostle Paul said that in the new man, which is the Body of Christ, there is no Greek, no Jew, no circumcision, no uncircumcision, no barbarian, and no Scythian. This means that there is no natural person, no religious or unreligious person, and no cultured or uncultured person. The natural person must be put off. If you are a religious person, you also must be put off. Some of us are still so religious. But in the church there is no circumcision or uncircumcision and no religious or unreligious. Many have the concept that as long as we are religious, it is sufficient. But in the church there are no religious people. The religious are really dreadful; they are a real damage to the church life. But the unreligious are even more dreadful. There is no circumcision or uncircumcision and no religious or unreligious in the church. There is also no Scythian. *Scythian* refers to those who are highly cultured. Culture or education, just as religion, means nothing in the church. Race means nothing, religion means nothing, and education means nothing. Whatever you are means nothing, and whatever you have attained means nothing. Do not think that you are something in the church because you have the highest attainment in education and religion. You must listen to the word of the apostle. In the new man, the Body of Christ, there are no Gentiles and no Hebrews, no religious and no unreligious, no cultured and no uncultured. All of these must be put off.

If we have never learned how to put off, we may be very active in the church, yet we are not functioning. There is a great difference between activities and functions. Activities are natural; they are something either of religion or of culture. In the church life we do not need activities. We need the functions which are the flow of life, the manifestation of Christ. It is not something of religion, nor of culture or education. We all must learn to put off all these things. Everything of religion, everything of culture or education, and everything of natural ability must be put off.

As a Christian, we may have learned how to be adjusted or corrected, but I am afraid that we have never learned how to put off. We must simply put off ourselves. We must put off our religion, and we must put off our education. Only then can Christ flow out. When we put off what we are and have, our natural being, our religion, our education, we can function and express Christ, who is the very life-giving Spirit indwelling our spirit.

FUNCTIONING MEMBERS

After we have been captured by Christ and are willing to grow in Him, we must learn how to put off all that we are and follow Christ within our spirit. Then we will become a functioning member in the Body, not just an active one.

The practical expression of the church is the local church, and in the local church there is the need of the functioning members. We do not have any clergy or laity, but we are all members of the Body. Therefore, we all must function. None of us should come to the Sunday morning meeting with the concept that we are going to "church." What are we going to "church" for? Is it to attend "the service"? A service requires a church building with people sitting in the pews, a pastor to preach a sermon, and a choir to sing specially arranged music. We are absolutely against this. If anyone comes to us with this kind of concept, they are in the wrong "store." They had better go elsewhere; we are not for this. We have no church service, no pews, no ministering pastor, and no choir.

Then what are we doing here? We are simply putting off religion, putting off Christianity. In the early days the church had to put away Judaism. Today we have to put off Christianity. For this, we all must change our concept. There is no pew, no pew members, no laymen, and no pastor. There are only the functioning members of the living Body. We all need to be captured by Christ, to grow in Him, and to walk in Him by putting off whatever we are and whatever we have attained. Only then can we become functioning members in the church to express the fullness of Christ in His Body.

THE MYSTERIOUS CHURCH

We all must realize what a local church is. The local church is a group of believers who are the living members of Christ, who forget what they are, and give up all their attainments to walk daily in the spirit. No outsiders can understand what we are doing. It seems that we are quite religious, but in fact we are not religious. We are not in religion. All outsiders find it difficult to understand us because we have something so hidden. The Lord in whom we live is so hidden. He is hidden within us; yet to us He is so real and so practical.

How can you explain this to outsiders? Since they and we are absolutely in two different worlds, how can they understand what we are doing? If they can understand, we must be wrong. Then we are of the earth. As long as we are a mystery, we are right. The more mysterious we are, the more we are right. The Lord does not need a religious people, but a mysterious people. Everyone among us should not be religious, but mysterious. Apparently, we are Christians, yet we put off Christianity. Apparently, we are quite religious, yet we are not of the world of religion. This is really a mystery. Praise the Lord! A Christian should not be an understandable person, but a mysterious person. The church is altogether a mystery, because all of us function as living members of the Body of Christ. We have given up all that people can understand. All that the world estimates of value, we put off, and we put on something which no one in this world can understand. It is something mysterious, yet so real.

BOLD IN FUNCTION

We do not want "pew" members; we want functioning members. So we all must be bold to function. We do not need to be bold in activities, but bold in functioning. The more we exercise our arm or any other part of our body, the more it will be strengthened, for the more blood that member will receive. So the more we function, the more we will enjoy Christ. The more we function, the more function we will have. Our function will increase all the time by functioning.

There is a brother in the church in Los Angeles who has been very active in functioning since the day he was saved six months ago. We all need to be like this. We must forget about our religious education. We all have some Christian background that has influenced us: we are used to coming to the church and sitting as pew members. But here is a brother who was one hundred percent a Gentile, without any influence of Christianity. After he was saved in the church, he immediately began to be a functioning member. I have encouraged him to function more, and we all must function too.

If we are going to function properly in the local church, we must be captured by Christ and then grow by opening ourselves and giving Christ more capacity to occupy and fill us. Then not only must we learn to put off worldly and sinful things, but also all our religious and educational attainments. Finally, we need simply to walk in the spirit day by day and hour by hour. There is no argument, no reasoning, no self-taste or self-choice. It is simply Christ Himself as all and in all.

To be in the spirit is not a matter of right and wrong; to be in the spirit is a matter of Christ. So we must learn to walk in the spirit and put off all that we are and have. Then when we come to the church meetings, we must be bold to function. We must not think much but simply function by releasing our spirit to express the Lord. Then we will grow in our function and be stronger and stronger, richer and richer.

May the Lord be merciful and gracious to us that the church here will be full of members who are so living and aggressive to function that Christ may be expressed in the spirit. This is the reality of the church life.

CHAPTER SIXTEEN

FUNCTIONING BY THE RELEASE OF THE SPIRIT

Scripture Reading: 2 Cor. 3:6, 17; Rom. 1:9; 8:4-5; 12:11; 1 Cor. 5:3-4

The real function in the church is the release of the spirit. The functioning in the local church depends entirely upon the release of the spirit. "The Spirit gives life" (2 Cor. 3:6). This is another basic principle.

"THE LETTER KILLS"

In our function, we must release the spirit. "The letter kills, but the Spirit gives life." *The letter* means doctrines, forms, regulations, and even ways or methods. All these things are letters. Anything other than the Spirit is a kind of letter, and the letter kills.

All of our function in the church must be out of the Spirit. It must be a release of the spirit. If we pray in the meetings, we must do it with the release of the spirit. If we share a testimony, we must do it in the release of the spirit. It must not only be *in* the spirit, but with the *release* of the spirit. Even when we go to visit a person for fellowship, we must do it with the release of the spirit. There must be the release of the spirit, because it is the Spirit who gives life.

Anything other than the Spirit is a kind of letter. We should not say that because I prayed in a certain way last night, I must do it that way all the time. This is something of the letter. It might have been living last night, but it will be dead this time. Last night it was in the Spirit, but now it becomes a kind of letter because the spirit is not released—only the way is kept. Even keeping the old way is of the letter.

The basic principle is that in all the function of the church, we need the release of the spirit.

You may ask whether you should pray loudly or silently, but I cannot say. If you can pray loudly with the release of the spirit, you must do it loudly. If you can release the spirit by praying silently, then do it. There is no regulation. Perhaps yesterday I had to pray loudly, but this morning I have to pray silently. The Spirit sometimes blows so strongly and sometimes so silently. We should not have any regulation according to a certain way. It all depends upon the release of the spirit.

Others may ask whether we should call for a hymn first or pray at the beginning of our meetings. But do not talk about first or second. If you put these things into regulations, they are immediately in letters. It all depends upon the release of the spirit. If you have the sense to pray at the beginning of the meeting, you must do it; then the release of the spirit will be so prevailing. There is no need for you to wait for a hymn to be called. If you think that you should not pray because a hymn has not yet been called, you will simply kill yourself and the others. The letter kills. This is why we are fighting against formal Christianity. The leaven of formal Christianity has even crept into the meetings of the local churches.

In some of the local churches, people are used to regulations. People come in and sit, waiting for the time to start. Then they wait for someone to call a hymn. Of course, these matters are not in writing, but they are written more deeply in their mind. If anyone behaves or functions in the meetings in a way which is not according to pattern, they say it is wrong. But this is of the letter. We must not only reject this but fight against it. We must fight against formalities.

We praise the Lord that the church in Los Angeles is somewhat peculiar. But I believe that we are not yet peculiar enough. We need to be more peculiar. I expect some day to see the brothers and sisters singing hymns on the streets as they are coming to the meetings. They will start to sing hymns and call on the Lord while they are driving in the car on the way to the meetings. They will even march into the hall with a hymn. Everyone will be so happy, fervent in the spirit, and set on fire. There will be no regulations, no forms, yet no disorder. Everything will be in good order, but in the spirit, without any regulations.

Some say that the church in Los Angeles is "awful." But it is still not "awful" enough! We need to be more "awful." We want to frighten all of Christianity to such an extent that the whole universe will be shaken.

Look at the picture on the day of Pentecost. Within Judaism something unusual occurred that day, which I am certain was not according to the regulations of the temple. I do believe that the Lord will do the same today. Praise the Lord! Today there is something new and different, something so peculiar and strange, happening to Christianity. Yet it is so spiritual, so living, and so full of life.

THE PRINCIPLE OF INCARNATION

We need to coordinate adequately with the Lord. In the New Testament dispensation, the Lord needs the human coordination. If we do not render any coordination to the Lord, the Lord cannot do anything, for in the New Testament dispensation there is the principle of incarnation. The principle of incarnation is that in everything God is mingled with man, and man is mingled with God. Man must cooperate with God before the Lord can work. I believe that the Lord has been waiting for a long time, even for nearly twenty centuries, for a proper coordination from man.

Do you not believe that the Holy Spirit is desirous of having a group of people singing on the streets? Do you think that the Holy Spirit is happy when so many Christians are dumb all the time? I do believe that the Lord desires Christians singing on the streets as they come to the meetings, and I believe that for centuries He has had this desire, but it has never occurred because the human coordination was lacking. If the Lord needed a kind of angelic coordination, this would have been done long ago. The angels would be so quick to afford an adequate coordination to the Lord. But we are so slow, so dull, so sloppy, and so influenced by formal religion that we think that it might not be so nice. Only a "bunch of fools" would sing on the streets as they come to the meetings.

We must learn to cooperate with the Lord. To do this, we must learn to walk in the spirit. The word *walk* in the Greek language means to do things, to say things, to behave and to have our being, including all the matters of our daily life. We must walk in the spirit. This means that we must have our being in the spirit. We must continually behave in the spirit. Even when we talk to our wife, we must talk in the spirit. We must not only pray in the meetings in the spirit, but even talk with our wives in the spirit. Then our spirit will be so exercised and strengthened.

Any part of the physical body needs proper exercise. Even our mentality, psychologically speaking, needs exercise. Those with a doctor's degree have exercised their mind for many years; therefore, they are so keen in their mind. But now we need the exercise of the spirit so that our spirit will be strengthened and made strong. We do have a spirit, so we must exercise and use it. Then not only will our spirit be made strong, but we will be so accustomed to using it. Then whatever we do or say will be done or said from the spirit.

What we need is not to wait for the inspiration of the Holy Spirit but to exercise our spirit. The Holy Spirit is waiting for us to exercise our spirit. It is similar to opening a window: when we open it, immediately a draft comes in. If we close the windows and doors and kneel down to pray for a draft, we are utterly foolish. "Lord, I am calling on You for the draft; I am waiting for You, Lord. I cannot do anything, Lord, unless You give the draft." This is an illustration of the wrong teaching in today's Christianity. I have seen people waiting for thirty years, yet no draft has come in.

The current of the draft is there, but He is waiting for the open windows. We must render the draft adequate coordination. If we simply open all the windows, Hallelujah, the draft comes in. If we exercise our spirit, the Holy Spirit will immediately move; He is waiting within us. So we must use and exercise our spirit all the time.

I believe that this point is clear, but we need much practice. Sometimes saints will ask how to overcome their temper.

Formerly, I told them a certain way, but today I simply tell them to exercise the spirit. If you are going to lose your temper, you must exercise your spirit to lose your temper. Everyone knows that if they will just exercise their spirit, they will not lose their temper. That is the way to overcome our temper. If we are going to overcome our temper, we must exercise our spirit. We must even exercise our spirit to laugh or to weep. All the time we need to practice this one matter of exercising our spirit in order that it may be strengthened. This will prepare us to coordinate with the Holy Spirit.

THE BREAKING OF THE OUTER MAN

Brother Watchman Nee has written a book entitled *The Breaking of the Outer Man and the Release of the Spirit.* I am afraid that many Christians who read this book will think that the release of the spirit means the Holy Spirit. This is wrong. Brother Nee meant that our spirit must be released. The Lord Himself as the life-giving Spirit is within our spirit. Our spirit is simply the container of the Lord as the life-giving Spirit. If our spirit is released, the Lord, who is within our spirit, will be spontaneously released. But if our spirit is closed, we imprison the Lord. He is confined in our spirit.

It is a fact that the more cultured a person is, the more self-conscious he is. Those who are not so well educated and cultured simply do not have much self-consciousness. If we are cultured, we are so careful to keep our standard. Whatever we say or do must be done in a proper way according to our standard. This just kills the spirit and builds up the outer man. All those who are cultured have a strong outer man. We all need the breaking of the outer man; the natural man must be broken. When we are in the meetings, we must function without any self-consciousness.

I was saved through the preaching of a young sister of about twenty-five years of age. She was speaking in a large meeting, which was attended by more than one thousand people. According to her natural disposition, she was exceedingly shy and self-conscious. But when she stood up to speak, she simply forgot about herself. You could sense the release of her spirit. She was not a good singer, but frequently in her preaching, she would sing songs. When she sang, the whole audience was convinced and even controlled by the release of her spirit.

We need to forget about ourselves. When we come to the meetings, we must even forget whether we are American or Chinese. We must simply be in the spirit. In some places I have met some highly qualified sisters. In all the meetings they kept their high standard. They were so highly qualified educationally, spiritually, and mentally. They had a high standard, and whenever they came to the meetings, they liked to keep it. Oh, how much they need to forget their standard so that they may learn how to release their spirit.

The natural man is the stronghold that imprisons our spirit. When the Lord Jesus as the life-giving Spirit is confined in our spirit, there is the need for breaking. Brother Watchman Nee told us that in preaching the gospel, the first lesson is to lose our face. This simply means to abandon our self-consciousness. Then the spirit will go out to reach the people. The principle is the same for functioning in the meetings. We all need to forget about ourselves; then the spirit will be released.

We still have many considerations which cause us to be bound. "Where the Spirit of the Lord is, there is freedom" (2 Cor. 3:17). So where there is no freedom, there is bondage of the spirit. Our natural disposition needs to be broken. Some brothers are very quick. But when they are quick in their natural disposition, this is a bondage to the spirit. Their quick disposition must be broken. Some brothers and sisters are very slow. This slow disposition also must be broken. We all need to learn the lesson of brokenness.

DEALING WITH BONDAGES

We all know that it is very easy for our spirit to be bound by sinful things. Anything sinful, anything worldly, or anything of the self and the flesh will immediately bind our spirit. Many brothers and sisters cannot say anything when they come to the meetings. They do not have one bit of release of their spirit. This is simply due to the fact that they are sinful and worldly and in the self and the flesh. Being sinful, worldly, and in the natural life binds the spirit. By dealing with all our sins, the world, and our self and flesh, we will immediately see the release of our spirit.

When I was away from Los Angeles recently, I heard that the brothers and sisters here had a big burning at the beach. Over a hundred people went there to burn all the sinful and worldly things. No one told me, but I believe this caused a real release. In such a case, when you sing Hallelujah, the tune is different. Without the release, the singing is not as good; but with the release, it is wonderful, for all bondages have been broken. Jesus breaks every fetter. Then there is the release of the spirit.

It is not only a matter of walking in the spirit and having the natural man broken; it is also a matter of dealing with all sinful, worldly, and fleshly things in the natural life. All these things are fetters, and we need by His grace to get rid of them. If we are a worldly church, we will be "pew" members, because everyone will be greatly bound. It is impossible to release the spirit. We must overcome all sinful things, all worldly things, all things in the flesh, and all things of the natural life. The more we get rid of these, the more we are released.

Of course, this will create a battle with the enemy. I heard that after the burning here in Los Angeles, there was a battle. The enemy, the subtle one, the evil one, came in to accuse, saying that too much had been done. But is it too much to get rid of all bondage? No! The more that is gone, the better. The enemy knows it. He utilizes the worldly things, the things of the flesh, and the things of the natural life to bind, to damage, and to wreck our spirit. When we are worldly, we are wrecked in the spirit, and as long as our spirit is wrecked, regardless of how much we love the Lord, we are finished. Many dear brothers and sisters have been wrecked by the enemy's subtlety so that they are simply useless. We must look to the Lord's mercy, that by His grace we will deal with all sinful things, all worldly things, all things of the flesh, all things that satisfy the self, and all things of the natural life. We can never do too much in this matter. The more we are purged, the more we are purified and released.

APPLYING THE BLOOD

One of the main principles in functioning is that we must never forget to apply the blood of Christ. It is the cleansing blood, the prevailing blood, and the victorious blood. Regardless of how much we deal with sinful and worldly things, we still need the cleansing of the blood. Whenever we are going to function, we must immediately apply the blood. "Lord, cleanse me once more, regardless of whether I sense that I am sinful or not. Cleanse me with Your precious blood. I praise You that where the sprinkling of the blood is, there is the anointing of the Spirit."

Look into the type of the Old Testament. With any kind of service rendered to the Lord by the priest, there was always the sprinkling of the blood. Every time we come to the meetings, we must come under the application of the cleansing and prevailing blood. We must declare to the whole universe that we are released, not because we are so pure, but because we are cleansed by the blood. We can say, "I am fully released, I am powerful and bold in the spirit, not because I am so right, but because I am under the prevailing blood." If we do this, we will see that even this declaration is a release of the spirit.

We know the subtle one too well. He has been our bad friend for years. Many times when you are burdened with something to share in the meeting, Satan comes in to damage. Just before the meeting, at the dinner table, your dear wife offends you a little, and you say something. Even if you say nothing, you are offended within. Then on the way to the meeting, Satan points out how defeated you are. He says, "Are you going to share something? A person like you?" We must realize that this is the evil, subtle accusation of the enemy to wreck our spirit. If we take it, either we will not share in the meeting, or we will share without the release of the spirit. Instead, we must declare to the enemy Satan that we know his subtlety. "Yes, I am a failure, but praise the Lord, I have the prevailing blood! I do not come to the meeting by my victory but by the blood of Christ." This declaration will put Satan to shame.

Whenever we come to the meetings, we must apply the blood. Satan is so subtle. He is always trying to damage, wreck, and spoil our spirit. So we need the cleansing of the blood all the time.

PRAY-READING THE WORD

The best way to have our spirit released is to pray-read the Word. This is because pray-reading the Word exercises our spirit and does not give us time to use our mind. The principles of pray-reading are to pray-read the Word in a quick way, with short phrases, praying something new and fresh. This keeps us from our mind and exercises our spirit. We know that the words of the Bible are living and full of nourishment. When we are pray-reading the Word in this way, our spirit becomes nourished, quickened, and refreshed. Thus, by pray-reading the Word, our spirit is exercised and strengthened.

Those of us who have pray-read the Word can all testify that this is the best way to practice the release of the spirit. We do not want to force anyone, but we want to help them to release their spirit. According to our experience, pray-reading the Word is the best way to release and exercise our spirit.

Because the function of the church requires a strong spirit, pray-reading the Word is most beneficial. It is the best way to strengthen our spirit. By pray-reading the Word, we can accomplish many things. With this one "stone," we can "kill many birds." So we do encourage others to pray-read the Word.

We must practice all these things so that our spirit may be released for the church life. If we are going to have a proper and living church life, we must function with the release of our spirit.

CHAPTER SEVENTEEN

FUNCTIONING BY PRAY-READING

Scripture Reading: Deut. 27:14-26; Rev. 5:9-14; 19:1-6; 1 Cor. 14:16

In the last chapter we mentioned the release of the spirit. Without the release of the spirit, there is no real function of life in the church. We may have certain functions of teachings, doctrines, and knowledge, but we cannot have any function of life if there is no release of the spirit. This is because "it is the Spirit who gives life." The function of life in the church requires the release of the spirit, and we have found by our own experiences that the best way to release the spirit is by pray-reading the Word. To find a proper way that really is effective in releasing our spirit, we must try pray-reading the Word.

SAYING AMEN TO THE WORD

We need to see something more regarding the pray-reading of the Word. The pray-reading we have had in the past is still not adequate. When we pray-read, we deal with the Word of God. We as human beings are very dull and slow when we come to the Word of God. We may be intelligent in reading scientific or philosophical books, but when we come to the Bible, we are blind. Something may be clear and definite in the Bible, but we may read it again and again, study it diligently, and even make careful research without seeing it.

Have you ever noticed that in Deuteronomy 27:14-26 the people say Amen to the Word of God twelve times? We must say Amen to the Word of God. The people of God in the Old Testament were even ordained by God to practice this. They had to say Amen to every word at the closing of God's Word in this chapter. Have you ever heard God's people say Amen to His Word? There are nine blessings in Matthew 5—"Blessed are those." Have you ever said Amen to these blessings? I have been a Christian for more than forty years, and I have never heard this.

Some may say that this is something of the Old Testament. But in 1 Corinthians 14:16 the apostle Paul tells us to pray with clear words that others might say Amen to our prayers. Moreover, the saying of Amen is not just something done on earth, but also in the heavens. Revelation 5 says that when the Lord Jesus ascended into the heavens, the heavens were filled with Amen. Revelation also shows us that in the future there will be a great Amen in the heavens. It is not just a matter on earth, but also in the heavens.

NOT ONLY SINGING BUT SAYING

Have you ever seen a church on the earth doing this? You may say that you have seen quite a number of churches singing, "Amen, Hallelujah." But that is singing, not saying. In Revelation 5 and 19 it is saying, not singing. It is not a kind of singing but a kind of saying. Have you ever seen Christians gathering just to say, "Amen, Hallelujah"? I have heard Christians singing, "Amen, Hallelujah" many times, but I have never heard a group of Christians saying, "Amen, Hallelujah!" What must we say Amen to? We must say Amen to the Word of God. Have you ever heard or practiced this? I believe that the Lord will lead us to do this.

Suppose we were to read Ephesians 4:4-7. When I read, "One Body," you all will say, "Amen!" When I say, "One Spirit," you all will say, "Amen!" And when I read, "One hope," you will say, "Amen!"..."One Lord"..."Amen" and so on. I believe that would be marvelous! Let us come together to Amen the Word of the Lord. When we open the Bible, we can say Amen to every word. When we say Amen to the Word, it will release the spirit. Take any book, any chapter, any phrase, and read. Then say Amen to what you read.

Sometimes we should let the sisters read and the brothers say Amen. At other times, we can have just four brothers stand up and read, and all the rest say Amen. When we have a large congregation, we can have ten read, and all the congregation say Amen. I believe they are already doing this in Taipei. There they have an enormous crowd to say Amen.

Without mercy, grace, and heavenly enlightenment, we cannot see this. But, praise the Lord, we do have this enlightenment. Why do we only use hymns to praise the Lord and not the Bible also? The Bible is full of praises. We must learn to say the Word together, to pray-read the Word together. We not only need to *sing* the music, but to *say* the words. That means to pray-read the words. I do believe that after pray-reading the Word in this way for a short time, our spirit will be released. It is wonderful, and it is so good. We do not need to compose anything; it is composed already. We only need to pray-read and say Amen to every part of the Word.

O LORD, AMEN, HALLELUJAH

We love to say the four words *O Lord, Amen, Hallelujah!* In the verses from Revelation, we have seen *Amen* and *Hallelujah*. Where then can we find *O Lord*? This is in the Psalms. In many pages of the Psalms, it is so easy to find *O Lord*. Therefore, these four words are not something we have invented but something we have discovered in the Word. When reading the Psalms in the past, we may have entirely passed over these two little words *O Lord*. If we use these two words and pray-read the Psalms again, it will be a new book.

The last five psalms, Psalms 146—150, all begin and end with *Hallelujah*. This means "Praise the Lord." Therefore, these five Psalms are called the Hallelujah Psalms. Every psalm begins with *Hallelujah* and ends with *Hallelujah*. So, in the Psalms we have *O Lord* and *Hallelujah*. We all must exercise ourselves to say these four words: *O Lord, Amen, Hallelujah!*

THE NEED OF PRACTICE

In learning to do anything, a certain amount of practice is necessary. At the beginning it is not so convenient, but by practice we gradually learn how to do it. I believe that we will gradually learn how to pray-read the Word in a better way. We are still at the beginning. If you regulate anything at the beginning, you will kill it. We must let it grow. When a little plant grows, you should not touch it too much. If you regulate it, you will kill it. But you should gradually adjust it a little. In the same way, our pray-reading of the Word will gradually need a little adjustment.

For instance, sometimes we do not take care of others when pray-reading in the meetings. We all say something at the same time. At other times everybody stops. Thus, we lack balance. This is because our technique is not yet so adequate. We have not practiced enough so that we have a balanced and coordinated pray-reading. We may have a living pray-reading but not a balanced and coordinated pray-reading.

We need practice, but we must not regulate too much. Do not make a form out of anything. We are living persons with some regulations yet with nothing formal. We need to acquire some skill and technique. Sometimes basketball players who are well coordinated play slowly and then suddenly play very quickly. In the same way, we may pray-read quickly and then slow down a little. Sometimes we may pray-read loudly and then silently, and sometimes we may have the leading of the Lord to all read together and say Amen. The main thing is practice. It takes practice to be perfect.

Another thing we have learned from our experience in pray-reading is that at the beginning all may pray together at the same time for about two minutes. This is like the sound of many waters, the voice of mighty thundering. But after two or three minutes, we should pray-read one by one. Then when we hit a strategic point, everybody may pray-read together loudly, but after a few minutes, all the voices will calm down again to pray-read one by one. It is similar to playing the piano: not every key is struck at the same time. Some are struck softly while others are struck loudly. This makes beautiful music. Our pray-reading should be like this. In the beginning we all pray together, but gradually we pray-read one by one until we reach a crescendo. This requires coordination. There are no regulations, but we all need to practice.

THE BALANCE OF THE SPIRIT AND THE SOUL

This does not mean that we do not need the teaching of

the Word, but it is more important that the spirit of all the saints be released and nourished. The messages are mostly to open our understanding. This is helpful, but it does not nourish and feed the spirit as much as pray-reading. We need the feeding, the releasing, and the stirring up of the spirit. In every meeting, we must first release and feed the spirit of the saints. Subsequently, we may have some message from the Lord to open our understanding. We not only have a spirit but also a soul; hence, for the spirit we need the pray-reading, and for the soul we need the understanding to be opened to the Word. This is the right way to be balanced. I do not mean that we do not need any solid and living teaching, but teachings alone are not adequate.

Why do we always say that it is not teachings we need but the Spirit? We say this because Christianity stresses teaching too much and neglects the feeding and nourishing of the spirit. Everyone can pray-read, but not everyone is a teacher. Some have the teaching gift, but most do not. Even a short message cannot be given by just anyone; yet everyone can pray-read. The whole congregation must pray-read. By doing this, the priesthood in the church will be greatly helped and strengthened.

THE WEAKER VESSELS

There is another matter regarding the pray-reading that must be mentioned. That is, the sisters must exercise a little boldness. Because the brothers are bold, it is rather difficult for the sisters to get a chance to pray-read. I noticed that in the sisters' meetings there is no problem. The sisters are bold in that kind of meeting, but in the regular meetings of the church, the sisters must be more bold and enter quickly into the pray-reading. The brothers, however, must sympathize with the weaker vessels and share the time with them. But the brothers must not wait too long; otherwise, the meeting will be deadened. We all must learn to "season" the meeting. Of course, this requires practice.

I believe that the Lord as the living Spirit will lead us in many ways. Henceforth, we are in the stage of the Spirit. We must give up our background, leave all the old ways, and follow the life-giving Spirit. He is so living; He is ever fresh and ever new. This will cause a real release of the spirit in the function of our meetings.

CHAPTER EIGHTEEN

THE GOVERNMENT OF THE CHURCH

Scripture Reading: 1 Pet. 5:1-6; Heb. 13:17, 24; Rom. 12:8; 1 Cor. 12:28

In this chapter we must look into another aspect of the local church, that is, the government of the church. With any government there are always two sides: the responsibility and the authority. We should not only have the thought of authority when we speak of government, because authority is not the only nor the first thing. The primary matter in government is responsibility. Without responsibility, there is no authority. The brothers who are in the government of the church must realize that they are not to exercise their authority but to take up their responsibility.

THE ELDERS

If we read through the New Testament carefully, we see clearly that in the local church there must be a government with elders appointed by the apostles (Acts 14:23; Titus 1:5). The Bible tells us that the elders are the leading ones. Hebrews 13:17 speaks of "the ones leading you," and Romans 12:8 speaks of "he who leads." So the elders are the leading ones.

We must realize that the elders in the local church are the leading ones. Have you ever seen a flock of sheep? A flock always has some sheep who take the lead; all the others follow the leading sheep. This is the real position of the elders. They must take the lead in the move of the flock. A good shepherd knows how to deal with the flock. There is no need to deal with the whole flock, but simply to deal with the leading ones. When the leading ones take the lead, all the rest will follow. The elders must be the leading ones in the local church.

TODAY'S ABNORMAL SITUATION

Today we are absolutely in an abnormal situation. Let me illustrate: Suppose a family, a father and mother with twelve or fourteen children, are all brought up properly and normally. In such a proper and normal family, it is easy to move in an orderly way. But now, in so many places, the beginning of the church life is not in such a normal condition. It is just as if the father and mother had died, and out of fourteen children, many have left home, and eventually only four come back to try to build up a proper family. Perhaps the oldest is only about eighteen years of age, with one sixteen, one fourteen, and one twelve. This is the present situation in the church life. In so many places there is no father, no mother, no big brother, no big sister, and almost all the elderly ones have left. Sometimes they may come to visit in order to criticize a little, but that is all. In this kind of situation, what shall we do? Should we say that since we have no father, mother, big brother, and big sister, we must forget about the family and wander on the streets? No, we must come back. Yet by coming back, we are all teenagers, and one is only twelve. But by His mercy and grace, we must come back to be the family. Many times the youngest, who is only twelve, is the wisest, while the oldest, who is eighteen, is not so wise. Sometimes, of the four who came back, the wisest is a sister; none of the three brothers can compare with her. But to let her take the lead is not so proper. In many places it is just like this. Those who should take the lead just cannot do it, but the sisters, who should not take the lead, are quite gifted and qualified. This is the real problem; it is absolutely abnormal.

In some places the brothers are much improved in the spirit, but they are under the influence of such problems in their background as being married twice. Of course, these things were in the past and are under the blood, but still the problem is there. A local church must be of a high standard. For some of the leading ones to be those who have a problem in the past is not good. So in this kind of abnormal situation we need more grace and more experience in life. It is just like the family of four children coming together to practice the family life. They realize their pitiful situation, yet they must come together as the family. How can they? There is a way. The oldest should realize that though he is the oldest, he is not the wisest. On one hand, he must take the lead, for no one else has that position, but on the other hand, he must learn to trust in his sister, knowing that she is much more capable than he. The two of them then become one. He is responsible for the position, and she is responsible for the ability. The sister realizes that she is more capable, yet she does not have the standing. So on one hand, she must be faithful to the family, but on the other, she must be willing to be covered by her brother. If she says anything, she must not say it directly, but by her brother. The brother does not know what to say, but she does. So through coordination she supplies the ability, and he takes the standing. They work together.

In many places among the brothers and sisters, hardly one is equipped both with standing and ability. Some have the standing without the ability, and others have the ability without the standing. Perhaps a brother who is very keen and much improved in the Lord has had two marriages before he was saved. He is really one with the Lord, and among all the brothers he is the most improved in the spirit. But how could he get rid of that blot on his history? It is always there, and because of the standard of the church, it is evidently not good for one with such a background to take the lead.

Some may say that others then should take the lead. But perhaps he who has the standing is just like plain water: he is neither sweet nor salty; he cannot do anything. If you ask him to take the lead, he simply cannot do it. So we need more mercy and grace, with more experience in life. These two brothers must work together. The one with the most improvement in the spirit must realize that though he has such an amount of spiritual ability, he has apparently lost the standard. He must realize where he stands and be faithful to the Lord in a covered way to be one with his brother. He must be faithful to God's grace and never take the lead, for he realizes his standing has been lost. If he would take it, he would damage the church and lower the standard of the church. He must therefore in faithfulness to the Lord do whatever he can to support his brother and be one with his brother.

The plain brother, then, must realize that though he has the standing, he is not capable of bearing the responsibility. Though he may be willing, yet he does not have the ability; so he needs the other brother. These two brothers must therefore become one. This is not so easy. They really need the mercy and grace of the Lord with much experience in life. If the one who is spiritual and improved in the spirit considers the brother in the lead and says that he is not qualified, the whole church life is gone. He must be one with his brother.

We all must realize that we are definitely in a kind of abnormal situation today. We all must look to the Lord for more experience in life. Today, in this time of abnormality, scarcely one among us is much qualified and equipped. Hence, several need to be one. A brother may have the standing and that is all. If he must make a decision, he must come to two other brothers. If he must say something, he will not know what to say; therefore, he must come to these two brothers and pray with them. He becomes their mouth, and they become his light—the three become one. This is the remedy for today's abnormal situation.

Moreover, we should not make the government in the churches so legal. We should not say that since these are the elders, let them do the job right or resign. This is wrong. If we have this attitude, it will damage the church life. We must realize that though the present leading ones may not be so qualified, we should not be so legal. They are still the leading ones; so let them take their position. We should do all we can to support them. There is no need for a change; we should do everything we can to help them.

Also, the leading ones must realize that they are not so capable. They should not make the situation so legal in such a way that everything must be in their hands. This is also wrong. Here we need the mercy and grace of the Lord.

Everyone among us must be faithful to the Lord, and everyone must learn that we do need the government in the church. I may be more capable than all those who are in the government, yet I realize that under the Lord's sovereignty I am not in the government. Therefore, I become so submissive to the government. Though the leading ones in the government are not as qualified as I may be, yet I do whatever I can to support them. I should not have any thought that some day the Lord will remove the present leading ones, and I will be one of the leaders. No, I should be submissive to the present government and support it. This is the attitude we should take.

The leading ones must realize that they should not control anything in the church in a legal way. This does not mean to surrender the order, but it does mean that there is no legality. Everyone is in grace. For instance, in some places, the leading ones think that because they are the leaders, they must start the meeting; if the leaders have not yet arrived at the meeting, no one should start. If some of the others begin the meeting, the leaders become angry. They like to hold everything so legally in their hand. This is wrong.

Then there are others who say that the leading ones restrict the Holy Spirit. They feel that everybody can do anything they like according to the Holy Spirit; therefore, they do not need leaders. This also is wrong.

I have been so happy with our meetings here in Los Angeles. We do not have any regulations in our meetings. Everyone is free to start the meeting, but there is no kind of disorder. I believe that this is right. If you say that there is no government, I will say strongly that there is a government. If you say that the church in Los Angeles is out of control and everybody is so free, I will say that the church in Los Angeles is very much under control. But if you say that there is a government with a certain kind of control, I will not admit this. There is no control. I will say a hundred times that no one controls.

What I mean is this: We do have a government here, but we do not have a legal government. We do not like to have anything legal; neither do we like to have anything in disorder. We like everything to be in order. We like everything to be in order, but not with legality. This requires more and more grace.

A CHANGE IN LIFE

If we all have learned the lesson of grace, wherever we go, we will simply go to the church on the proper ground. Then when we get into that local church, we will submit ourselves to the situation and not question anything. By the Lord's leading we will do our best to minister life to others and support the government of the church. This will build up the church and give ground to the Lord for Him to do something more.

When King David was young, he was in an abnormal situation. But he learned the lesson, and this paved the way for the Lord to come in. Therefore, the Lord was able to put him into the position of king. If we have the grace and learn the lesson of life, someday the Lord will put the responsibility on our shoulders. He will bring us into the government of the church. *But this must be the sovereign move of the Lord, not something brought about by our manipulation.*

In the church any replacement or change in the government may cause a loss. We do not need an outward change, but we do need a change in life. Perhaps in the church in certain places, the leading ones are not as qualified and as living as you are. But you must be faithful to the Lord to minister life, submit yourself to the leading ones, and do whatever you can to support and help the present government. This will minister more life to the whole church, and this life will bring about a change in life. Perhaps after a few more years, spontaneously some of the present leaders will be moved by the Lord. Then in life you and some others who are experienced in life will be put into the leading position by the Lord. It will not be something done by human hands, but by the sovereign, divine hand. It will be something in life, and it will not cause any damage to the church life.

CHAPTER NINETEEN

THE CONTENT OF THE CHURCH

Scripture Reading: Matt. 13:3; 1 Cor. 3:6-7; 1 Pet. 1:23; 2:2, 5; Eph. 2:21; 4:15-16

What is the content of the church? Some may answer that the content of the church is Christ. This is right; but when people say "Christ," sometimes they do not understand what they mean. Christ is the content of the church, but we must realize that this Christ who is the content of the church is life to us. He must be our life in order to be the content of the church. Christ does not merely come and stand among us as the content of the church; it is not in this way. As such, He would only be the ruler of the church, not the content of the church. If He is to be the content of the church, He must be our life. The content of the church is Christ as life to us. All Christians recognize that Christ is in the church, but few realize that Christ in the church means that He is life to us. He is not only in the midst of the saints, but He is also life to the saints as the content of the church.

When we say "life," we must realize that life can never be separated from the Spirit. The Spirit is the reality of life, and the Spirit *is* life itself. Thus, when we say that Christ is life to us, we must realize that this life is in the Spirit. Christ is the life-giving Spirit in our spirit. He could never be life to us except in the divine Spirit, and we could never enjoy, realize, and experience Him as life unless we are in the human spirit. It is in the human spirit that we realize and experience Christ as the life-giving Spirit. It is not just the teaching or talk about life but the real experience of life. This is why we stress that we must turn to the spirit and know how to exercise our spirit.

It is similar to our relationship to the air. Our physical body has its being in the air. Air, in a sense, is life to us, but we need to breathe it. By breathing the air, we can realize the air as life. In the same way, it is not by understanding or knowing but by exercising our spirit to breathe that Christ as the life-giving Spirit can be realized as our very life.

NOT GOOD BUT GOLDEN

Suppose there are two brothers in the church. One is a nice man by birth, not by regeneration: he was born nice and gentle. It is difficult for him to lose his temper; it even seems that he has no temper. Regardless of what you say or do, he is never offended. He seems to be in another world, a world without a temper. He has an exceedingly gentle disposition. Now he is saved and is one of the brothers, and everyone thinks that he is a wonderful brother.

Another brother, on the contrary, can so easily lose his temper. He is not so refined, but indeed quite rough. Everyone in the church is afraid of him, especially the sisters. They are afraid of his tough disposition and his capacity to easily lose his temper.

Suppose we have these two brothers in the church. One is "white," and the other is "black." I am not referring to the color of their skin but to their disposition. Which would you love, the black one or the white one? Suppose one of these two brothers were going to stay with you. Which would you like to have? Would you take the white one and give someone else the black? Which would you choose? It depends on how much you want to be transformed. Undoubtedly, the black one would contribute more to your transformation. But the answer is that we should prefer neither of them. We should not love the white or the black, for both are natural. Neither of them is of life. One is white, but he is not "golden." The other is black, and he is not "golden" either. What God wants is "gold," not white or black. Good is not "gold," and neither is bad. Regardless of whether you are white or black, as long as you are not "golden," God will not take you.

The church is not a place for the education or correction of people. The church is not a place to change people. It is the very means for God to put Christ as life into man. The black ones need life, and the white ones also need life. But according to the situation of today's Christianity, this is not so. Today's Christianity attempts to educate, correct, and change people. If you are white, they say that you are all right. But if you are black, they try to correct, change, and improve you. This is absolutely wrong. The content of the church is nothing less than Christ as life. The black ones are undoubtedly short of Christ, but so are the white. All are short of Christ.

Many times the white ones become a real frustration to life. In many local churches, the black ones are easier to handle as far as life is concerned. To minister life to them is easy, but to minister life to the white ones is really difficult. The white ones think they are quite all right, and others also think they are good. Within them there is a certain kind of pride in being better than others. All the brothers and sisters think that it is unnecessary to pray for them; they think that they must pray for the black ones. So eventually, the white ones become a frustration to the ministry of life. It is difficult to convince the white ones that they need Christ even more.

THE WAY OF HELP

How can we help these two brothers? Suppose the black one continually loses his temper and is so rough with the brothers and sisters. What shall we do? Most people will try to convince him that he is wrong. They will condemn him, and if he is slightly convinced, they will rebuke him. Sometimes they will rebuke him to death. Finally, they will ask him to correct and change his attitude—"Brother, you know that in the church we must have a life of love. You should not behave yourself in such a poor way. You must conduct yourself in love and learn to love others." This is what most people do, but it is absolutely wrong.

Suppose such a brother comes to you, what would you do? According to my experience, the best way is not to condemn and adjust him but to minister life to him. Pray-read a part of the Word with him, and bring him into the presence of the Lord. After a certain amount of pray-reading and contacting the Lord, you may say something to him in a positive way.

"Brother, we are all sinners. Good does not mean anything to the Lord—even our best does not mean anything to Him. What the Lord wants is just Himself as our life." By saying this, you are not political, and you are not vindicating or condemning. You are out of the world of good and evil, and in another world, another sphere, another realm, which can help him to realize Christ. He is so concerned about being right or wrong, but you must stay in the other realm to help him to realize that neither good nor evil mean anything to God. You have to bring him out of the sphere of good and evil and into the sphere of Christ, which is the sphere of life. Of course, it will take time. You will have to contact him again and again, but always in the principle of bringing him out of the sphere of good and evil and into Christ as life.

Gradually and daily in this way, you will feed this brother with Christ. You must feed him little by little and never condemn or rebuke him. Simply feed him with Christ as life. Whenever he comes to you, you should never speak of who is right or who is wrong, who is proud or who is humble. You must give him the impression that you do not care for this. To act nicely or poorly means nothing, but Christ as life means everything. Gradually you will bring him into the full realization of life. Then he will realize that it is unnecessary to fight against his bad temper and disposition. He will forget about this. He will turn to the spirit to contact and enjoy the Lord.

TRANSFORMED, NOT CHANGED

Eventually, this black brother will be transformed. He may be transformed into a transparent black stone. He may still be black, but transparent. Have you never seen a precious stone which is black, but transparent? It is a beautiful stone. I do like to see the black brothers transformed. They are black, but transformed. I have also seen some white brothers transformed to be so crystally transparent.

Do not think that those of a quick disposition are better than those of a slow disposition, or visa versa. They are all the same. Some precious stones are white, and some are black. The color of some you cannot tell—you do not know whether to call them white, black, blue, or some other color; yet they are beautiful, precious stones. Some of the brothers are just like this. They are not so quick, and they are not so slow. They are just something of beauty. We do not need to be changed, but we all need to be transformed. Do not try to change others. They are God's creation; why do you want to change them? We do not like to have a church with everyone uniform—so nice, and in a sense so humble, yet so dull. We need a variety of colors in different kinds of people. This is the beauty of the church.

Some brothers and sisters are so simple and easy to handle. Others, however, are so complicated and difficult to manage—many times I simply do not have patience with them. But I have learned to see the beauty. We all must realize that the church is not something to correct, to rebuke, or to change. No, the church is the very means to minister Christ to all kinds of people so that they may be transformed with Him as life.

Let me use another illustration. Suppose a sister simply cannot go along with her husband. The other sisters realize that she is a problem in the church life because she has a problem with her husband. What is the proper way to help her? The regular way in Christianity is to show love to her and convince her that she is wrong by the teaching in Ephesians 5. First, you should love her, and then you should try in a nice way to convince her from Ephesians 5 that she is wrong in her relationship with her husband. This is the usual way. It is not bad, but as far as Christ as life is concerned, it is wrong. If you have such a sister among you, you must learn the real lesson of life. *It is not submission that pleases God, but it is Christ as life expressed in submission.* This is what God is seeking. If you have learned this lesson, you cannot expect to be through quickly with this sister. You must care for her day by day, little by little. You must continually give her something of life till she is brought to the full realization that what she needs is not a kind of submission but Christ as life expressed in her submission to her husband. Then she will know that it is not a problem of being submissive but of experiencing Christ as life. The sisters should not try to change or correct this sister but minister Christ as life to her.

THE SEED OF LIFE

How did the Lord Jesus begin the church life? Some people have the concept that Christ began the church life with teaching. No, He did not do that. The Lord Jesus began the church life by sowing Himself into man as the seed of life. The church life simply comes out of this very seed of life. The Lord Jesus came to sow Himself into us, and this seed of life brings forth the church life. Matthew 13:3 says, "Behold, the sower went out to sow." The Lord Jesus came not as a teacher to begin the church life by teaching but as a sower, sowing Himself as the seed of life into the fallen race. It is from this seed that something springs forth as the church life.

The apostle Paul says, "I planted, Apollos watered" (1 Cor. 3:6). Do not imagine that Paul went simply to preach and Apollos came to teach. No, Paul planted, and Apollos watered. Both planting and watering are for the growth of life, which issues from the seed which is Christ Himself. I like these three words: *sowing, planting,* and *watering.* What the local church mostly needs is not teaching but planting and watering. We do need to be watered that we may grow. Teaching does not help us to grow, but watering does. This is why it is rather difficult for anyone to see a real church life on the earth today. It is simply because of the lack of planting and watering among the Christians. Teaching alone kills and divides, but watering helps the growth.

First Corinthians 3 speaks of the church being planted and watered and also mentions something more. It says that we are not only the farm of God but also God's building. The farm requires the growth, and the building requires the building up. We can be built up by growth. If we want a solid church life with a group of believers built up in a solid way, we must minister Christ as life so that everyone will grow. First Corinthians 3 speaks of the growth and the building up. It is by growth that we can be built up together.

First Peter 1:23 tells us that we were all born of the incorruptible seed, which is Christ, the living Word. Christ has sown Himself into us as this seed, and out of this seed we are born. After we are born, as newborn babes, we need the milk of the word in order that we may grow unto salvation (ch. 2). We need to be saved from so many things, and this kind of salvation can only be realized by growth in life. This corresponds with Romans 5:10, which tells us that we must be saved in His life. It is by growth in life that we are saved.

We need milk, not knowledge. The newborn babes need to drink of the milk that they may grow. Then 1 Peter 2 continues by saying that as we grow, we become the living stones to be built up together. The more we grow, the more we grow *together*. The more we grow, the more we grow into one. The more we grow, the more we grow into a building. We are built up together by growth, not by being organized or taught. It is all by growth in life.

Wherever we go, we must not try to adjust others. Let them be wrong. Do not try to correct and change them. What they need is to grow. Even if you can adjust and correct them, it means nothing, for there is still no growth in life.

THE GROWTH IN LIFE

What is required in the church is the growth in life. I do not expect to see any change in the brothers, but I do expect to see growth. Sometimes you can see growth with certain brothers or sisters, but it seems that there is no apparent change. Do not be concerned; the change will appear later. Change by the growth of life does not come quickly. Outward correction brings swift results, even overnight, but this is not of life.

Anything of life grows very steadily, yet very slowly. Anything human is manufactured and is done very quickly. You can make a man of wax in less than two days, but you cannot make me within two days. Do you know how long it took to make me as I now am? It took over sixty years, and I am still in the process of growth. This is the law of life. We should not expect a brother to change overnight. If he does, the change is not the change in life.

Sometimes I hear Christians testifying of a brother who becomes another kind of person overnight. But in another night, he may become a third kind of person. This is too fast. Life grows steadily but in a slow way. We need patience to go on with those in the church and let them be what they are. Sometimes we may have to wait for more than twenty-four or even thirty months before we see a real change. All the mothers expect their children to grow, but it takes time. If you look at them today, they seem to be the same as yesterday. If you look at them tomorrow, they are about the same as today. But after ten years, there is a great change. This is the growth of life.

In the church we need the real growth of life. We expect a quick change, but we must be patient and help people to grow, not in the way of teaching, but in the way of life. Sometimes there are those who really trouble the church, but let them be so troublesome. Do not be bothered by that. Be patient, and let them grow. Simply minister life little by little. Praise the Lord! After five years you will see the growth.

All the brothers here can testify that in all these past years, we have not exercised much correction. But praise the Lord, look at the growth in life! The growth in life is all we need. It will take care of everything. It transforms us instead of simply changing us. Ephesians 4:15-16 shows us that the real building of the Body is by growth. "Holding to truth in love, we may grow up into Him in all things." This "causes the growth of the Body unto the building up of itself in love." It is by this growth that the Body is built up.

In every local church there is a certain amount of problems and troubles. This is because children always cause problems, and every local church has so many children. But we must not be bothered. To have problems in a family with so many children is normal. If you have four children without any problems, I doubt whether your family is normal. That means that all the children are dead. The more alive they are, the more troubles you will have. Do not be so troubled with the problems in your locality. Praise the Lord, it is normal!

We must learn how to feed on the Lord and how to feed others. We do not need much teaching, so we should not give much teaching to others. By His mercy and grace, we must help others to realize that they need Christ as life all the time in a practical and living way. Then in time, we will see the growth.

THE TASTE OF LIFE

The content of the church is not any kind of capability or qualification. In the church we do not need those who are capable. In the church we need Christ as life experienced by a group of people. We need those who know only one thing— Christ as their life. They may seem so simple, so foolish, and even so troublesome; yet there is the sense of life. It is rather difficult for you to define it, but there is this sense.

We cannot define life, we can only taste it. If you can tell people about the church in Los Angeles in a clear, defined way, I am afraid that we are just an organization with many activities, but without life. But if you say, "Praise the Lord! Hallelujah! When I was in Los Angeles, I tasted something wonderful which I cannot define," this is right. If others ask you what you have tasted, you can only tell them to go and taste for themselves.

The church in every locality must have such a taste of life. Others must sense that nothing is here but Christ as life. It is so living, so enjoyable, and so tasteful. There is the sense, but it cannot be described. Everyone must taste for himself.

Therefore, we must not bring anything into the church. Neither should we create something in the church as a kind of content. The content of the church is nothing but the living Christ as life to all the members.

CHAPTER TWENTY

BUILDING IN LOVE

Scripture Reading: Eph. 4:16; 1 Cor. 8:1; 1 Cor. 13

In this chapter we must see that love is the practical living of the church. The church's living is love. The word *living* can also mean expression; the expression of a local church is love. If we only demonstrate a certain kind of teaching or form, we are wrong. The expression of the local church must be love.

THE MOST EXCELLENT WAY

Why did the apostle Paul write 1 Corinthians 13? Chapters 12, 13, and 14 are three chapters forming a section which deals with gifts. The middle part is the chapter on love. The church at Corinth had left the proper expression of the local church: they had turned from love to the exercise of gifts; they had become a kind of manifestation of gifts rather than love. The first thing seen at Corinth was the practice of gifts—mainly, the speaking in tongues. The apostle Paul then wrote and adjusted them. Tongues and other gifts are not the most excellent way. Only love is the excellent way, and in a sense, love is the best way. At the end of chapter 12, the apostle Paul says, "Earnestly desire the greater gifts. And moreover I show to you a most excellent way" (v. 31). What is the most excellent way? The answer is in the following chapter, that is, love. He opened the next chapter in this way: "If I speak in the tongues of men and of angels but do not have love..." (v. 1). This verse proves that tongues and other gifts are different from love. We may have the gifts and still lack the love. We may speak in the tongues of men and of angels and still be short of love. If so, we are as sounding brass or a clanging cymbal. There is the sound but not the love; the noise but not the life.

I have been concerned for many years because some Christians pay too much attention to tongues. They have neglected this verse, which tells us that speaking in tongues is not something in life. Tongues are only a kind of sound. They are not life. Sound without love proves that speaking in tongues is not of life. Otherwise, the apostle would not speak in this way. He opened this chapter by saying that the Corinthian believers need life, not just sound. What is the expression of life? It must be love, for life is expressed in love. Love is not sound; love is the expression of life.

We must never try to love by our own strength. I am not encouraging you to love, because I know that you cannot love. The more I exhort you to love, the more you will hate. The more I demand love from you, the more I will get hatred from you. We simply cannot love. We can do many things, but we cannot love. It is easy to speak in tongues, but it is not so easy to love. Love is the most excellent way; therefore, it is the most difficult way.

The greatest difficulty in the church life is love. We can teach, but we cannot love. We can serve, but we cannot love. We can clean, but we cannot love. We can mow the lawn, but we cannot love. The sisters can play the piano, but they cannot love. It is easy for us to pray-read, but we cannot love. We simply cannot love. It is easy to do anything but love.

THE DESCRIPTION OF LOVE

What is love? If we read the description of love again in this chapter, we will realize that Christ is love. Love is Christ Himself. "Love suffers long. Love is kind; it is not jealous. Love does not brag and is not puffed up; it does not behave unbecomingly and does not seek its own things; it is not provoked and does not take account of evil" (vv. 4-5). Love is a person. The whole description of love in this chapter pertains to a living person, and that person is Christ.

What can exist forever and ever? Only Christ. In this chapter the apostle Paul minimizes all things but love. Nothing can compare with love. All the offerings, donations, and gifts cannot compare with love. Even prophecy and knowledge cannot compare with it.

First Corinthians 13:8 says, "Love never falls away. But whether prophecies, they will be rendered useless; or tongues, they will cease; or knowledge, it will be rendered useless." Paul uses these two phrases in this verse: *rendered useless* and *cease*. What will be rendered useless? Prophecies and knowledge. What will cease? Tongues. Tongues, prophecies, and knowledge will be rendered useless and cease. The Word is exceedingly clear in this verse, but many so-called Pentecostal groups simply pay all their attention to prophecies and tongues. Love never falls away. Prophecies will be rendered useless, tongues will cease, and knowledge will also be rendered useless, but love remains forever. Who is this love? It is God Himself. God is love. What can compare with God? Tongues? Prophecies? Knowledge? No! Only God is eternal.

"Knowledge puffs up, but love builds up" (8:1). Christians think they need the teachings, but this is wrong. We should not put too much trust in teachings or gifts. We must put absolute trust in love.

In the first of the seven epistles in Revelation, the Lord Jesus says that they had lost their first love. The word *first* in Greek also means "best." The first love is the best love. *Philadelphia,* the church to whom the sixth epistle was written, means "brotherly love," and this is the best of the seven churches. The best church is the church of brotherly love, not the church of gifts, knowledge, or power. The Lord only wants a church of love.

THE WRONG CONCEPT

I do not believe that the Lord will use the gifts very much in His recovery. He will reveal Himself to the seeking ones as life, and this life will be expressed in love. It is not a human kind of love. This love is simply God Himself, living in us and expressed through us.

We must abandon the concept that gifts are the only requirement for the building up of the church. Gifts alone and, even more, the teachings cannot build up the church. Teaching divides and causes division. Every denomination has been established by a teacher. Church history shows that whenever and wherever there was a great teacher, there was a division. Teaching divides, but love unites and builds up. The only thing that builds up is love. But the love of which we are speaking and the love the Bible teaches is not human love. This love is God Himself; so to realize this love, we must relinquish all other things. We should not trust in anything but love for the building up of the church. We should not put our trust in gifts or teachings.

Some have been teaching for years, but where is one genuine church built up by teaching? Christianity is not new; it has been here for centuries. But where is the church built up by teachings? History shows that teachings and gifts have not been effective in the building up of the church. We should never put our trust in these things, but rather in love. The Lord be merciful to us that we may drop all distracting things and come back to love—just love. We all must realize that nothing can build up the church but love. Ephesians 4:16 tells us it is in love that the Body builds itself up. But the problem is that we are so religious and natural. We still have the concept that we need teachings.

Others condemn us and say that we are exclusive and do not accept all ministries. But if we were to invite the best speakers on earth to come and speak to us, the church would simply be a mess. Suppose we have twelve good, spiritual, sound, and fundamental teachers speak to us every month for a year. I am afraid that by the next year, the church would be gone. Only love edifies and builds up the church. It is not merely the gifts, the teachings, or the ministries that build up the church; it is love.

First Corinthians 13 says that even if I know mysteries and have all knowledge and prophecy, yet without love, I am nothing. As far as the building up of the Body is concerned, without love I am nothing. These things alone cannot build up the Body. We must all change our concept so that we do not put so much trust in teachings. The Body can only be built up in love. If we would love, we must give up many things of the teachings and gifts. We should not trust in anything more than love.

Look at the situation today. Where is the church that is built up by teaching? In the past nineteen years of experience in Taiwan, those who thought they had a gift of teaching became troublemakers. There was not one exception. They proclaimed that they had the gift, but they did not help the work much. The work was mostly carried on by those who did not claim to have a gift. They just learned to serve the Lord by being what they were. They did not consider themselves as gifted persons, but just served the Lord in love. Thus, we see that it is not the gift, but love. All the churches on the island of Taiwan do not have much trust in gifts, because by past experience they saw that all the trouble came from the so-called gifted persons.

If we are going to practice the church life, our concept must be one hundred percent turned. Do not trust much in any teaching or gift. They do not work so well. The real building comes from love, simply love. We must drop the concept that teachings, gifts, and other things can help much in the building up of the church.

A TESTIMONY OF LOVE

In the last chapter we stressed that the content of the church is life. But how can we prove life except by love? When we have a conference and training, I do not trust much in my ministry. This is simply the best time for the brothers from so many different places to come and taste the love. I would prefer to hear the visitors to Los Angeles say that they did not get much help from the ministry, but, oh, what hospitality and love they experienced among the brothers and sisters! We need a church life full of love. When others come, they should sense the reality of love. It is not just a matter of ministry, but the reality of life expressed in love. It is marvelous to have such a testimony. We thank the Lord that He has been gracious to us in this matter, but we need more. A strong testimony is a testimony of love. We do not have much trust in anything but love.

All the dear ones who are in the Lord's recovery should never have much respect for any gift or ministry. We should not have much trust in anything but love. Then we will see churches full of life and strength, without too much knowledge. This is what we need in the Lord's recovery.

The reality of the oneness mentioned in Psalm 133 can only come out of love, not out of any ministry. The more ministries we have, the more divisive elements and dissenting opinions we will have. We have learned this by suffering. You do not know how much we have suffered by inviting good speakers. It did not help the building up of the church. On the contrary, I cannot tell you how much damage it has caused.

The Lord has proved that the real need for building up the local church is love. But if we want to love, we must have our concept absolutely uprooted. I fear that we still have the concept that we need more ministries, teachings, and gifts. This concept must be uprooted. All we need is love. Love will bring in the building up of a marvelous church life.

ETERNAL LOVE

Knowledge and prophesies will be rendered useless, and tongues will cease. Only love remains forever. All the ministries and gifts will pass away, but love will remain for eternity. I do believe that in eternity many of us will remember the days spent in Los Angeles. Though eternity will be much better, still we will recall these days of love in Los Angeles. This is the real building.

Love never falls away, and love builds up. There is not much need of good speakers. We must be patient in going on by the Lord Himself as love in life. Then we will see the church gradually build itself up in love. The real expression of the local church life is life, and a church full of love is a church with a long life. All the so-called churches built up by ministries and gifts are short-lived; it is not long before they are divided. But the church that is built up by love never ends. Nothing can divide it, damage it, or touch it because of love. Love is the strongest bond.

My burden in this chapter is just to tell you that nothing but love can edify or build up the church. Where, I ask, is a church built up by teachings or gifts? We should not care for theory, but for the practicality. Teachings, gifts, or knowledge have never worked, but Christians are still trying them. They

have wasted years and years, but they are still trying. The
Lord be merciful to us that we may be willing to be delivered
out of this concept. All we need is God in Christ expressed as
love. Only this can build up the church.

CHAPTER TWENTY-ONE

THE INCREASE AND SPREAD OF THE CHURCH

Scripture Reading: John 15:4-5, 7-8; Phil. 1:27; Matt. 28:18-20;
Acts 1:8; 8:1

THE INCREASE OF THE CHURCH

In this chapter we must see the increase of the church.
The increase of the church is to impart Christ to others and
make them a part of Christ. The branches of the vine bear
fruit by imparting the life of the vine to others and making
them a part of the vine. If the branches of a vine do not bear
fruit, there will be no increase of the vine. The fruit-bearing
of the branches is the increase of the vine tree. So the
increase of the church is by the fruit-bearing of all the members. All the members must bear fruit; otherwise, there will
be no increase of the local church.

Today in Christianity, nearly everything is abnormal, even
the preaching of the gospel. Christianity today depends upon
the giant preachers with huge gospel campaigns, but this is
not so in the Bible. In the Bible, especially in the Gospel of
John, the real gospel preaching is the fruit-bearing of every
member. Here in Los Angeles the church does not have any
kind of gospel campaign, yet every month there are a good
number of new converts that come into the church life. It
seems that apparently there is no preaching of the gospel, yet
new ones are continually brought in. It is just like the tree of
life in the New Jerusalem: it bears new fruit every month.
This is the proper preaching of the gospel, and this is the
increase of the church. It does not depend upon great preachers and large gospel campaigns. The normal daily life of the

members of the church is simply to bear fruit; then there is the increase of the church.

The proper way to preach the gospel is to impart Christ into others as life. We should not trust in the great preachers; we have to trust in ourselves. Every member of the church is a branch to bear fruit. Consider the fruit tree. Every kind of fruit tree bears fruit at least once a year—this is a natural law. I do believe that as living members of the local church, we must bring at least one new convert a year to the Lord. Suppose a branch of the vine does not bear fruit year after year. What do they do with it? They prune it or cut it off. Every local church must encourage every member to bring at least one new convert to the Lord every year. Even to bring in ten or twelve a year is not too many, for that is simply like a cluster of grapes.

In the local church we should be fruitful. Whenever we come to the church meeting, we must come with some new ones. Do not come to the meetings alone—that is not a glory; that is a shame. We need to come to the meetings with others for the increase of the local church.

Some of the young brothers here in Los Angeles are of Japanese origin and were recently saved. They were not saved by gospel-preaching meetings, but through the daily contact of members of the church. This is the proper bearing of fruit.

THE WRONG CONCEPTS

In the gospel preaching, there are some wrong concepts that I must point out to you. In some of the denominational churches there is much activity in the outreach of the gospel. This is good, but the problem is that there is too much human effort and struggle. This is wrong, but this does not mean that we should retire from fruit-bearing and not bear fruit. We should not be old in bearing fruit; we should always be renewed. There is no retirement in the spiritual life.

Another kind of concept in Christianity is that we must wait and pray for a great revival—then the Lord will send a giant speaker, and we will come together to have a gospel campaign. This is abnormal. In the last chapter I mentioned that we should not trust much in the teachers and ministers for the building up of the church. This does not work well. Now I say that we must not depend much on a large campaign for the gospel. This also is not normal.

There is a third concept—at the other extreme—which is also wrong. Some say, "Look at those people. All their gospel campaigns are just in the energy of the flesh." Of course, we must realize that all our gospel preaching must be the overflow of the inner life. But those who criticize in this way have been criticizing others for years, yet they themselves have not brought in any new ones. It seems that there is no overflow of life with them. So they have gone to the other extreme.

THE NORMAL WAY

What is the normal way? The normal way is not to use our human effort; nor is it to depend upon a revival campaign with a giant preacher. Fruit-bearing is the outflow of life; so we must grow in life and also take the responsibility of fruit-bearing. The church should encourage every member to pray for the bringing in of new converts to the church. We should spend at least two or three hours weekly to take care of some new ones. It is not right for a church to remain the same in number year after year. Suppose that after five years we still have the same number. This is absolutely wrong. This means that we do not have the exercise of the flow of life.

What do I mean by the flow of life? I mean that we must abide in the Lord and enjoy the riches of His life. Then we must be burdened for fruit-bearing. We must pray, "Lord, my daily life is to bear fruit." Then the Lord will give us a deep realization for two or three persons for whom we should care. We may know fifty persons, but at that time the Lord will burden us with only two or three. We will pray for them, mentioning their names to the Lord. Then we need to seek the Lord's guidance regarding how to contact them. Perhaps we will invite them to dinner along with some of the brothers and sisters; then there will be others to help in ministering life to them. The brothers and sisters in the church should help one another in a mutual way in the matter of fruit-bearing. We should not do this just once in a while but constantly. This is our daily life. We should spend at least two or three hours weekly in this matter. Do not expect a quick job. It is by doing it steadily and constantly that we will see the results.

If every year each one would bring in one new convert, within a year's time the church would be doubled, and after another year it would be doubled again. The young people should bring in one new one every six months. It is not too much to bring in one new convert in one hundred and eighty days. In fact, it is too little. If each one could bring in two a year, by the end of the year, the church would be doubled twice. This is the increase.

Some may say that this is too much. Suppose then that each one brings in one every two years, or that two brothers bring in one each year. In six years the church will have doubled three times. That is not bad. And you cannot say that it is too much for each one to bring in one every two years. What an increase there would be!

We must not trust in the big gospel campaigns; we must trust in the increase of the church. The increase of the church is the fruit-bearing, not a great campaign. As a branch we must bear fruit, and one fruit every two years is so easy.

LIMITATIONS TO THE INCREASE OF THE CHURCH

The increase and fruit-bearing of the church can be greatly frustrated and limited by the disposition of the leading ones in the churches. Some leading brothers possess a natural disposition against having many people. They always like to have around seventy-five or eighty in the church, and certainly not more than one hundred. This is their disposition. They like to be a leader of a small number, not a large one. If the number is too large, they feel they cannot handle it. This is why our natural disposition must be broken. In a city with nearly three million people like Los Angeles, how can we be limited to just seventy or eighty? We should expect to see one day in Los Angeles more than one hundred meeting halls, with a thousand brothers and sisters in every hall. Even that is not too many, for one hundred thousand is just three and one-third percent of three million. We need to be enlarged.

Do not condemn those who bring in twenty but lose eighteen. If you bring in twenty and lose eighteen, you still have

two left. It is better than nothing. Where are the ones you
have brought in? Eighteen may have gone, but there are still
two. How many do you have? However, I do not believe that
many will be lost.

Our disposition must be transformed. We must bear fruit.
In some of the places I have visited, I have cried silently to
the Lord, "Lord, be merciful to this place. They have been
here five years, and there is still no increase." This simply
has been due to the disposition of the leading ones. They did
not like to have so many. They were satisfied just with a mod-
erate number. The Lord be merciful to us that we may never
have such a disposition.

Some of the leading ones do not like to be so busy in taking
care of new ones. That is their disposition. This kind of disposition restricts the increase of the church. Do you know what
the Lord told us? He told us to go to the streets and the
byways and force people to come in. We have to be aggressive
in this matter.

A few things are very necessary for the church life: to walk
and live in the spirit, to experience Christ as life, to take a
firm standing on the proper, unique ground, and to bear fruit
for an adequate increase. If there is a vine with many branches,
spontaneously fruit will be brought forth, and this will be the
real increase of the tree. I am not against any gospel campaign or any famous preacher, but the normal Christian
church life is that of every member bearing fruit. This is the
normal condition. It is unnecessary for the local church to
hold a large campaign. If a number of believers are meeting
and fellowshipping together week after week, month after
month, new fruit should spontaneously be brought forth. There
may be no preaching, yet new fruit is brought forth. This is
right. It is exactly similar to putting our trust in all the members, not in the teachings and ministries, to build up the
church. In the same principle, to bear fruit we must trust in
all the members.

The leading ones of all the churches must be enlarged in
their disposition. It is true that to have more people is a kind
of trouble, but we must be enlarged. The leaders must learn
to share the responsibilities with others. But again, this is a

matter of disposition. Some of the leading ones do not like to have others share the responsibility; they like to have everything in their hands. This has to be broken if the church is to increase.

THE SPREAD OF THE CHURCH

Locally, it is the increase; universally, it is the spread. The church needs the increase locally, and the spread universally. If the church in Los Angeles has been existing locally for ten years without any increase, and there is still only one church in this country without any spreading, we are wrong. The church must be spreading from city to city. I expect that in the near future, there will even be an expression in Mexico City.

Some may say that this is contradictory to what I have said about being concentrated. No, it is for experience that we are concentrated to be trained. We come together for the strengthening of the testimony and that we might be trained and experienced. Then at a certain time, we will migrate out to spread the church life from city to city.

If we read the book of Acts carefully, we will see that the spreading of the gospel had two lines. The first line was the migration of the saints—not the going out of the apostles. Acts 8:1 says very plainly that all the saints were scattered abroad, except the apostles. We have always thought that the apostles had to go out and the saints had to stay. But the Lord scattered all the saints and kept the apostles in Jerusalem. The sent ones stayed, and all the others were sent out. This was the first spreading of the gospel. It was not by the apostles going but by the scattering of the believers. This is what we call migration. The spreading of God's kingdom really does not only depend on the apostles, but also on the believers migrating from city to city.

According to Luke 21:24, Jerusalem has been returned to the people of Israel. This is the strongest fact indicating that the time of the Lord's return is very near. Therefore, locally we must have the increase, and universally we must have the spreading. As a local expression we must have many saints going out. We are not here for our interest; we are here for the Lord's recovery. The time is near; the Lord is coming back. We must take care of His interest. We must look to the Lord that some will be burdened to go, and all of us should be willing to be burdened to go. We are the descendants of Abraham. Abraham was a stranger who continually sojourned on the earth. It is not right for us to be so settled in one place. We have to move from one place to another. We must be here for the Lord's interest. If we are here as a local expression of the Lord's Body without an increase locally and a spreading universally, we are wrong. We should not think that we are more spiritual than others. If we do, we are too proud. We must be so living and burning all the time for a certain amount of increase locally and for a measure of spreading universally.

We are living today in the richest country on the earth. Everything is so available, and we are in the very center of the populated world. It is exceedingly easy and convenient for us to go north, south, east, or west. We must spread the Lord's testimony to many cities in this country and Canada, as well as to Mexico, Central and South America, and Europe. We must look to the Lord that we will have such an increase locally and such a spreading universally.

CHAPTER TWENTY-TWO

PREPARATION FOR THE LORD'S RETURN

Scripture Reading: Luke 21:24-28; 1 Thes. 5:1-10

THE LORD'S MOVE IN CHINA

From 1920 in China, especially among the young people, the Lord began to do a marvelous work. The gospel was brought to the educated circles, and many young college students from the north to the south were brought to the Lord, among whom was Watchman Nee. I was saved through the preaching of these young people and came in just a few years later. Soon after that, the Lord began a real move for Himself and His church in China. It began when people were helped to be clear regarding the assurance of salvation. Before that time, many had been brought into Christianity, but very few were clear concerning the assurance of salvation. If you went to the Christians in China at that time to ask whether they knew they were saved or not, you would find that most of them would not know. They thought they had to wait till they died before the Lord would tell them whether or not they were saved. But praise the Lord, He raised up a good group of young Chinese Christians under the leadership of Brother Watchman Nee, and the matter of the assurance of salvation was made very clear.

Then the Lord began to show us that Christ is life to us. We saw that Christ not only died on the cross for our sins, but also to put us to an end. Christ died that we might be brought to an end and that He could be life to us; then we could live by His resurrection life. Christ as life to us was made very clear, and we all learned the lesson of how to live by Him. It was at that time that the messages of *The Normal Christian Life* were given in China. Of course, some years later, in 1938 and 1939, these messages were given again in Europe by Brother Nee and have now been compiled and published as the present book.

In those days, after people became clear regarding the assurance of salvation, they were helped to realize that Christ lives in us to be our life. Then the Lord began to recover the church life. From the very beginning, the Lord showed us these three things: the assurance of salvation, Christ as life, and the church life. From that time, wherever we went, we had no other burden but these three matters. We simply did not have any burden to speak of anything but the assurance of salvation, Christ as life, and the church life. Hardly anything was said about prophecy.

THE START IN THE UNITED STATES

Then the Lord began something in this country and brought us here for His testimony in 1962. We realized that it was unnecessary to take care of the assurance of salvation, because so many Christians in this country are already quite clear about this matter. Therefore, in the past few years we have concentrated on two matters: Christ as life, and the church as the expression of Christ. We have never touched the matter of prophecy in our ministry in this country.

JERUSALEM RETURNED TO ISRAEL

In this chapter, however, I feel that the ministry must be turned a little, because the age has been turned. Have you realized that from the summer of 1967, the world situation has really changed? Before June of that year, Jerusalem, the holy city, was fully trodden under the feet of the Gentiles. Now all the people on earth realize that in June of 1967 the people of Israel gained a real victory. By just a six-day war, Jerusalem was returned to Israel in a miraculous way. When I heard the news, I was greatly excited, for I knew the prophecy in Luke 21:24. The things prophesied by the Lord Jesus in Luke 21:20-24 were mostly fulfilled at the time of Titus, the prince of the Roman Empire, in A.D. 70. When Titus took over Israel, Jerusalem was completely and thoroughly destroyed.

Many were killed, and the rest were scattered. This is predicted by the Lord in the first part of Luke 21:24: "They will fall by the edge of the sword and will be led captive into all the nations." The last part of Luke 21:24 says that "Jerusalem will be trampled by the Gentiles until the times of the Gentiles are fulfilled." This was the reason I was so excited when I heard the news that Jerusalem was returned to Israel. More than forty years ago I learned of this prophecy, and now I have seen it fulfilled. Just overnight, Jerusalem, which has been fully trampled by the Gentiles for nearly twenty centuries, was returned to the people of Israel. If we read Luke 21:24-28, we will realize that this is the first and greatest sign of the Lord's return.

When I was a young Christian studying these things, I believed the Word of God. But still in my mind there was a question. Could Jerusalem really be returned to the people of Israel? Could this be possible? It seemed to me at that time that it was impossible, but now we all know that Jerusalem has been returned. Is not this marvelous? This is the first sign of the Lord's return.

THE WAY FOR THE LORD TO COME BACK

Luke 21:24 has now been fully accomplished. But how can the Lord come back? If we read the entire New Testament, we will realize that there must be a group of people on this earth who have been regenerated, transformed, built up together, and prepared as His bride for Him to come back as the Bridegroom. The Lord is returning to judge the earth, but this is not His goal. The main purpose of the Lord's return is for His bride (Rev. 19:7-9). To judge the earth is on the negative side, but to come for His bride is positive.

In 1936 someone declared that the time had come for the Lord to return. But we knew that that was wrong, because the bride was not prepared. Now more than thirty-one years (up to 1967) have passed, and Jerusalem has been returned to the people of Israel. I do believe that henceforth the Lord is going to do a quick work to prepare a group of people by transforming them and building them together to be prepared as His bride.

We should not expect that all the Christians will be revived. That will not occur. The Lord will work according to the principle of the overcomers. This means that the majority of God's people will not prepare the way for His return. Only a remnant will go along with the Lord and by His mercy stand with Him to fight for His recovery. This is the principle whereby the Lord can do a quick work. If we must wait for the Lord to revive all the Christians, I do not know how long that would take. But it is easy for the Lord to raise up a small number of seeking ones here and there in all the earth. The Lord is going to raise up a small number to take the standing of the overcomers to go along with Him. These will be the representatives of His Body, and their standing will be sufficient to bring the Lord back.

Then the Lord will say, "Satan, look! You have done whatever you can to damage My church. Yet on this earth, here and there, a small number still stands with Me." This will pave the way for the Lord to return, and this will give Him ground on which to stand. If the Lord were to come back today, there would be no ground on which He could stand on the earth. But if a small number of the Lord's people were to be prepared, transformed, united, and built up as a local expression here and there, the Lord would have the ground He needs. He could say to Satan, "Satan, I do have a standing on this earth. The earth has rejected Me under your evil leadership, but now there is a group of people who will not go along with you. They have given Me the ground to stand on; so now I can return to regain the whole earth."

TODAY'S WORLD SITUATION

I believe that this is the Lord's burden today. As a seeker of Christ, we must realize that the world situation today is the real fulfillment of the Word of God. Not only the return o the city of Jerusalem but even the talks in the United Nations are part of the fulfillment. First Thessalonians 5:3 says, "When they say, Peace and security, then sudden destruction comes upon them, just as birth pangs to a woman with child; and they shall by no means escape."

Do you know what they are talking about in the United

Nations? It is nothing but peace and security. They talk continuously about peace and security. If you ask the politicians and statesmen why there is a United Nations, they will tell you that it is for peace and security. But the more they speak about peace and security, the more there is no peace and security. This kind of talk is also a sign of the Lord's coming. If we look into the world's history, there has never been such a period in which people on earth have spoken so much concerning peace and security. Have you realized that this is a sign of the Lord's return? The more they talk about peace, the more they do not have peace. The more they talk about security, the more the security disappears.

I have been watching the world situation day by day for about fifty years. Every year there is more talk concerning peace and security, but there is no peace and security. Nineteen years after World War I, in 1937, the second war began in Manchuria. In 1945 World War II was terminated, but the problem has never been solved. By 1968 World War II had ended twenty-three years previously, but the problem is still here. The first war was over only for nineteen years, but the second war still is not over. Everyone talks about peace and security, but there is no peace and security.

THE WORLD COMING TO AN END

The world is coming to an end, and the Lord is coming back. We are not children of darkness but children of light; so everything is clear to us. The people of the world are dreaming about peace and security, but it will never come. The Lord is coming back; so let us be wise and sober. Let the people of the world be foolish. While they are crying for peace and security, the Lord will return.

Brothers and sisters, how can we be prepared for the Lord's coming? First Thessalonians 5:9-10 says, "God did not appoint us to wrath but to the obtaining of salvation through our Lord Jesus Christ, who died for us in order that whether we watch or sleep, we may live together with Him." This corresponds with all the ministry in the past years. We must learn to live with Him, to be one with Him by always turning to our spirit. To live with Christ means to be one with Him.

Whatever we say, we must say together with Him. Wherever we go, we must go together with Him. We must simply be one with Him. In our home we must be one with Him. In school we must be one with Him. In our business we must be one with Him. We must live with Christ in our spirit. This is the proper way for us to be prepared.

If we will take this one step to live with Christ, we will immediately be turned. We will be turned to the heavenly way from the world. Jesus is near. Jerusalem has been returned, and the whole world is talking about peace and security. This is the strongest sign that this is the end of this age. The coming of the Lord Jesus is imminent. Therefore, we must be prepared by learning to live with Him, and we must be transformed and built up in a local expression of His Body so that we may be prepared as His bride for His return.

ABOUT THE AUTHOR

Witness Lee was born in 1905 in northern China and raised in a Christian family. At age 19 he was fully captured for Christ and immediately consecrated himself to preach the gospel for the rest of his life. Early in his service, he met Watchman Nee, a renowned preacher, teacher, and writer. Witness Lee labored together with Watchman Nee under his direction. In 1934 Watchman Nee entrusted Witness Lee with the responsibility for his publication operation, called the Shanghai Gospel Bookroom.

Prior to the Communist takeover in 1949, Witness Lee was sent by Watchman Nee and his other co-workers to Taiwan to ensure that the things delivered to them by the Lord would not be lost. Watchman Nee instructed Witness Lee to continue the former's publishing operation abroad as the Taiwan Gospel Bookroom, which has been publicly recognized as the publisher of Watchman Nee's works outside China. Witness Lee's work in Taiwan manifested the Lord's abundant blessing. From a mere 350 believers, newly fled from the mainland, the churches in Taiwan grew to 20,000 in five years.

In 1962 Witness Lee felt led of the Lord to come to the United States, settling in California. During his 35 years of service in the U.S., he ministered in weekly meetings and weekend conferences, delivering several thousand spoken messages. Much of his speaking has since been published as over 400 titles. Many of these have been translated into over fourteen languages. He gave his last public conference in February 1997 at the age of 91.

He leaves behind a prolific presentation of the truth in the Bible. His major work, *Life-study of the Bible,* comprises over 25,000 pages of commentary on every book of the Bible from the perspective of the believers' enjoyment and experience of God's divine life in Christ through the Holy Spirit. Witness Lee was the chief editor of a new translation of the New Testament into Chinese called the Recovery Version and directed the translation of the same into English. The Recovery Version also appears in a number of other languages. He provided an extensive body of footnotes, outlines, and spiritual cross references. A radio broadcast of his messages can be heard on Christian radio stations in the United States. In 1965 Witness Lee founded Living Stream Ministry, a non-profit corporation, located in Anaheim, California, which officially presents his and Watchman Nee's ministry.

Witness Lee's ministry emphasizes the experience of Christ as life and the practical oneness of the believers as the Body of Christ. Stressing the importance of attending to both these matters, he led the churches under his care to grow in Christian life and function. He was unbending in his conviction that God's goal is not narrow sectarianism but the Body of Christ. In time, believers began to meet simply as the church in their localities in response to this conviction. In recent years a number of new churches have been raised up in Russia and in many eastern European countries.

OTHER BOOKS PUBLISHED BY
Living Stream Ministry

Titles by Witness Lee:

Abraham—Called by God	978-0-7363-0359-0
The Experience of Life	978-0-87083-417-2
The Knowledge of Life	978-0-87083-419-6
The Tree of Life	978-0-87083-300-7
The Economy of God	978-0-87083-415-8
The Divine Economy	978-0-87083-268-0
God's New Testament Economy	978-0-87083-199-7
The World Situation and God's Move	978-0-87083-092-1
Christ vs. Religion	978-0-87083-010-5
The All-inclusive Christ	978-0-87083-020-4
Gospel Outlines	978-0-87083-039-6
Character	978-0-87083-322-9
The Secret of Experiencing Christ	978-0-87083-227-7
The Life and Way for the Practice of the Church Life	978-0-87083-785-2
The Basic Revelation in the Holy Scriptures	978-0-87083-105-8
The Crucial Revelation of Life in the Scriptures	978-0-87083-372-4
The Spirit with Our Spirit	978-0-87083-798-2
Christ as the Reality	978-0-87083-047-1
The Central Line of the Divine Revelation	978-0-87083-960-3
The Full Knowledge of the Word of God	978-0-87083-289-5
Watchman Nee—A Seer of the Divine Revelation ...	978-0-87083-625-1

Titles by Watchman Nee:

How to Study the Bible	978-0-7363-0407-8
God's Overcomers	978-0-7363-0433-7
The New Covenant	978-0-7363-0088-9
The Spiritual Man • 3 volumes	978-0-7363-0269-2
Authority and Submission	978-0-7363-0185-5
The Overcoming Life	978-1-57593-817-2
The Glorious Church	978-0-87083-745-6
The Prayer Ministry of the Church	978-0-87083-860-6
The Breaking of the Outer Man and the Release ...	978-1-57593-955-1
The Mystery of Christ	978-1-57593-954-4
The God of Abraham, Isaac, and Jacob	978-0-87083-932-0
The Song of Songs	978-0-87083-872-9
The Gospel of God • 2 volumes	978-1-57593-953-7
The Normal Christian Church Life	978-0-87083-027-3
The Character of the Lord's Worker	978-1-57593-322-1
The Normal Christian Faith	978-0-87083-748-7
Watchman Nee's Testimony	978-0-87083-051-8

Available at
Christian bookstores, or contact Living Stream Ministry
2431 W. La Palma Ave. • Anaheim, CA 92801
1-800-549-5164 • www.livingstream.com